How To Be an Outstanding Form Tutor

I0875890

Form tutors need to be the port in a storm, the defender, the challenger, the safe space, the ally, the consistent role model and efficient administrator. The role of form tutor changes over key stages and has an understated value in a secondary school's pastoral care system: they are likely to be the first adult in school to greet a child each morning, thereby potentially setting the tone for the day, and they are the go-to person for any problems that child encounters. This is the book many secondary school teachers wish they had had in training: a comprehensive guide on how to do much more than take the register and give out notices.

It is designed to persuade teachers at all stages of their career to invest time and energy into being an excellent form tutor. The book covers topics including:

- Attendance and punctuality
- Mental health and wellbeing
- Working with others
- How to teach PSHE safely and effectively

Guidance for first time form tutors, a source of renewed enthusiasm for seasoned professionals and a training manual for pastoral leaders, this one-stop shop for all form tutoring needs is an essential part of every school toolkit.

Sophie-Lauren McPhee is a former secondary school teacher and psychotherapist in training. Until August 2024 she held the position of Trust Lead Professional of PSHE & SMSC at The Mercian Trust and led PSHE at Queen Mary's Grammar School in Walsall, alongside running a private counselling practice for adults and couples and educational outreach: https://www.stoneymeadow.co.uk/

Andy Allman is an experienced secondary school teacher, who is currently the Curriculum Lead of Personal Development for Tadcaster Grammar School in North Yorkshire, leading on PSHE and RSE. He has previously been a Head of Year and an Associate Assistant Headteacher in state schools across England.

How To Be an Outstanding Form Tutor

A Guide to the Most Important Job in School

Edited by
Andy Allman and Sophie-Lauren McPhee

Routledge
Taylor & Francis Group
LONDON AND NEW YORK

Designed cover image: © Getty Images

First published 2027
by Routledge
4 Park Square, Milton Park, Abingdon, Oxon OX14 4RN

and by Routledge
605 Third Avenue, New York, NY 10158

Routledge is an imprint of the Taylor & Francis Group, an informa business

British Library Cataloguing-in-Publication Data
A catalogue record for this book is available from the British Library

ISBN: 978-1-041-02791-1 (hbk)
ISBN: 978-1-041-02787-4 (pbk)
ISBN: 978-1-003-62097-6 (ebk)

DOI: 10.4324/9781003620976

Typeset in Galliard
by Apex CoVantge, LLC

Contents

Contributors

Kelly Allchin is a UK-based personal development and careers education specialist with 20 years' experience in teaching, leadership and training. A former senior leader in Leeds, she led on personal development and careers education across her school. Now Education and CPD Lead at Pol-Ed, she writes resources, trains educators, and also works as an independent freelance consultant supporting schools' personal development provision.

Andy Allman has been speaking out for form tutors for several years now. He is an experienced teacher and middle leader, having worked in state schools across England for nearly two decades. A former Year Leader, a former Associate Assistant Head, and a lapsed history teacher, he is currently Curriculum Lead for Personal Development at Tadcaster Grammar School.

David Best is a teacher of mathematics and Head of Year 8 at Queen Mary's Grammar School, UK. He has been teaching for more than ten years in various types of schools. He also has an M.A. in Education that focuses on working with disadvantaged pupils. He has been a form tutor to all year groups in various tutor settings.

Kim Constable has over 20 years in education, specialising in Sociology and PSHCE, working as a sixth-form tutor for over a decade. Having worked in schools in London, UK and internationally, she currently teaches in a state boarding school. She has shared teaching resources under 'The Hectic Teacher' brand for 15 years, providing engaging materials to support teachers and reduce workload.

Sanum J. Khan is a senior leader at Sir Henry Floyd Grammar School in the UK, with her main subjects being RS and PSHE and leading on Personal Development. She regularly engages in educational research and evidence informed practice, including an action research project on the underachievement of Pakistani boys, and contributing to work on the retention and promotion of representative staff.

Mark McKie currently teaches mathematics at Tadcaster Grammar School, UK. Teaching since 1992, he was runner-up in Regional National Teaching Awards and has spent much of his career helping to bring the best out of both students and other teachers, as an Advanced Skills Teacher, Head of Department and mentoring beginner teachers. Outside of school he is a keen cyclist.

Sophie-Lauren McPhee is a former UK secondary school teacher with 20 years' experience, specialising in PSHE for the past decade. She has led PSHE at school and trust level and contributed to a number of publications, most notably as co-editor of *Developing Quality PSHE in Secondary Schools and Colleges* (Bloomsbury, 2024). She is also a trainee psychotherapist in private practice.

James Nichols is a UK-based former headteacher and teacher of history and politics with a vast experience of middle and senior leadership. He is now the Director of Political Education For Students (PEFS), which seeks to enthuse, engage and educate young people in politics, government, citizenship and democracy. In addition, he leads JSN Education, supporting schools, leaders and teachers to deliver excellence.

Olivia Saunders is an experienced leader specialising in safeguarding, inclusion and school improvement. A champion of pastoral leadership and character development, she focuses her work around ensuring every young person feels safe, seen and supported. She has worked in both education and charity sectors in the UK, advising on how schools and institutions can improve equity, wellbeing and meaningful progression opportunities for young adults.

Joshua Speer is a teacher, careers adviser and careers leader at Brighton, Hove and Sussex Sixth Form College, UK and is an experienced middle manager within pastoral support and personal development. Joshua has worked exclusively across the post-16 sector and is committed to developing young people across all aspects of their educational journey. Joshua's interests span philosophy of education and education policy.

Foreword

By Ross Morrison McGill,
former school leader, best-selling author and founder of @TeacherToolkit.

Want to See School Culture?

Start here. If you want to know what a school's culture is really like, don't start by reading its mission statement. Pop your head into a tutor room. Listen to the conversations. Watch the routines. Notice the relationships. In the first 20 minutes of the school day, you will see, in miniature, what the school truly values – standards, belonging, and pastoral care.

The routines, relationships and interactions taking place in this space will tell you everything about what is going on in the school. From managing expectations to completing the register, to 'checking in' on uniform mishaps and misdemeanours, to a quiet mental health 'Q&A' at the back of the room. Observe a form tutor going about the loud, quiet, difficult or beautiful moments when managing a tutor group, and you will see what makes teaching complicated, and the joyful vocation that it is.

The Most Powerful Job Nobody Trains You for

Without doubt, the most enjoyable role in a school isn't the one in the best-paid job, the teacher with the lightest timetable, or the person with the fanciest job title, it's the one that happens quietly, every morning, in the same room, with the same pupils, day after day.

I have always believed that the form tutor role is one of the most influential jobs in a school. It is the only role that sits at the intersection of standards, belonging and safeguarding – all at once. Lessons matter.

The curriculum matters. Outcomes matter too. But being a form tutor is where a teacher shows how they truly understand children, not just data.

Like any job, you can invest as much time and effort into the tutor role as you want, and the return on that investment is rarely immediate. A greeting at the door every morning, a quiet 'check-in' whispered in a child's ear as they sit with their head on the table, or that end-of-week positive phone call to let families know how well their child is doing. These are small, effortful choices a form tutor can take to establish routine, repeated without any drama. Yet, every tutor group is different.

Small Routines, Big Outcomes!

Some tutor groups are instantly cohesive and easy to shape. Others are fragile, loud and challenging, requiring many days and weeks of time and effort to restore some balance. Strong tutor routines protect learning for the rest of the day. Outstanding tutors ensure all pupils are known, and heard. They help pupils to manage their emotions, mental health and relationships. There is a great deal going on each morning which sets the tone for the rest of the day, and if this time is left to chance, it creates a hidden curriculum that becomes disposable. It teaches pupils that standards are optional from the first part of the day. What happens here is that this period of time is viewed not as an opportunity, but as time to set different standards, alternative to lesson delivery. Standards are negotiable, uniform standards become sloppy, and the small details, from equipment to 'reply slips', are checked, chased, done properly.

Why Some Tutor Groups Fly (and Others Fracture)

Over two decades, I was fortunate enough to support the pastoral needs of four different tutor groups, seeing two of these groups across the full five years of their secondary school experience. The first group I recall, was like managing a showdown in the Wild West. It wasn't necessarily that all the pupils were wild. Those challenges of being a tutor had more to do with the school leadership at the time, the trajectory of the school, and my tutor inexperience. I had zero support for the role as a teacher, as early career induction didn't exist when I qualified. So, what hope did I have of being a form tutor? I had to learn the hard way, surviving in most cases, and I let things slip that I now wish I'd handled differently.

The 949-days Commitment

My second form group was another chance at learning from what support I wasn't given, taking on the role from day one in a start-up school. Meeting excited parents, I remember vividly, and gleefully, telling parents to 'go home' the moment the morning bell rang in the playground. Thirty families 'shooed away' as I marched my tutees off to their tutor room. I couldn't wait to get started, and I spent the following 949 other days listening, building relationships, following-up on promises, dealing with difficulties, observing challenges, and managing family trauma to name a few. Supporting this group of 30 young people and their families was probably the highlight of my career.

In the other two tutor group experiences, as my leadership responsibilities increased, my form tutor experiences diminished. However, I tried to hold on to the role for as long as I could. In my second and third tutor group, I took on the role of 'buddying' another teacher to become a form tutor, sharing the role and responsibilities. This enabled me to deal with unplanned leadership emergencies, and support another teacher to become effective in the role. Prior to this, form tutor training was unheard of, rarely considered, with much left to chance. Academic calendars, pupil planners, checklists and family events were becoming more thoughtful, with a 'pastoral curriculum' increasing in importance, as much as profile, budgets were set aside to provide resources to help make tutoring, and being a tutee, successful.

The Joker Card

However, I also learned that over a sustained period of time, you cannot rely solely on classroom authority or resources. You need relational credibility, and this is your 'joker card'. This can manifest itself simply in all students knowing who you are, where to go to for help, you knowing as much as you can about each family, and them knowing who you are too. You are the first port of call. Interestingly, I was always surprised to learn that one or two pupils didn't know the names of other pupils in the tutor group, sometimes after weeks and months together, so I worked hard to mix seating plans, design activities, end of term parties and lunchtime clubs to facilitate friendships. This is the 'joker card.' It's that unforeseen moment in the future, where you use your influence for protection and progress, preventing exclusion, stabilising attendance, walking a pupil to an after-school club to help get a boost for their coursework grade, to reframing a pupil's self-worth as they navigate a new home, family member or difficult period. Your role as a form tutor can be the only person fighting a child's corner when things get difficult, and this social capital is not a trick. It's the product of your quiet consistency, developed every day across the year.

One Pivotal Moment

In the last form tutor role I experienced, the school I was co-leading took on the epic challenge of vertical tutoring. This involved placing all pupils in mixed-aged groups to provide more pastoral support by stage, rather than age. Suddenly, tutors, support staff too, were paired with pupils and exposed to all aspects of school life. Younger pupils found themselves observing older pupils select their GCSEs, and older pupils witnessed low-level conflict and self-doubt in younger pupils, offering guidance in structured conversations as part of a rolling timetable. Every form group across the building became a school microcosm, and all staff, including school leaders, could participate in all aspects of pastoral life, rather than only see, for example, the year eight experience. The shift was seismic, and school values were transformed using redistributed responsibilities. More adults, deeper pastoral knowledge, structured training, and greater collective ownership. It is probably one of the most impactful, leadership experiences of my career.

The Form Teacher Legacy

One of the simplest measures of impact isn't on a spreadsheet. It's whether pupils turn up every day, remember your name, or stand on a stage for the school performance after years of personal self-doubt.

Form tutors live at the meeting point of school systems and family reality. They deal with daily friction, missing PE kits, lost equipment, mobile phones, detentions, friendship conflicts, punctuality and so much more. They are also (often) the adult who is first to spot a safeguarding concern before it becomes a headline.

Some of the pupils I first tutored will be well into adulthood. Some have connected with me over the years to let me know how they are doing, sharing their personal and professional successes. I mention this carefully and generally, because the professional boundaries of being a tutor matter, but the point still stands: Tutoring can be the kind of long-view relationship that reminds you what schools are really for, and post-pandemic, with increasing absence, anxiety and home education, being an 'Outstanding Form Tutor' and knowing how to achieve this, matters more than it has ever done before.

Pupils don't remember every lesson. They remember who noticed them. They remember who is listening to them, and how you made them feel. When teachers are given the role of the tutor, the most effective don't give up this responsibility and view it as an additional workload burden. Instead, they view their role as a daily chance to make school feel coherent, safe and demanding in the right ways. One can start to get a sense of the impact small conversations an 'outstanding tutor' may have on the character development of a child, and well into adulthood. Some of my former pupils describe strong memories, decision-making and morals shaped by some of our short, 20 minutes together each morning. Any indelible footprint on a child is easily forgotten when you are dealing with uniform or bullying issues on a daily basis, and this is why I am proud to play a small part in this excellent book written by Sophie and Andy.

This Is Why Sophie and Andy Wrote This Book

How to Be an Outstanding Form Tutor is a timely contribution, providing schools with a detailed bank of pastoral concepts, ideas and resources. It covers topics from brain-based concepts, to identity, and relationships. The whole, encompassing role of school life, is supported by evidence-informed practice. This book is also essential for any teacher who finds themselves (like I once did) without any training or support – thrown in at the deep end! *How to Be an Outstanding Form*

Tutor approaches tutoring not as 'dead time' some may believe it to be, but the most important job in the school. Sophie and Andy show you how to achieve the role of a tutor, successfully, with intention and ambition. I only wish I had a copy of this book when I started tutoring in 1997!

Introduction

Andy Allman

Picture this. My second placement in my teacher training had just begun. I wasn't particularly confident at that stage, and wouldn't be particularly competent either. My department was excellent, the school leadership was superb, and I was put in with a Year 9 form group in a Science room. So far so good . . . until by the end of the first week when it's clearly transpired that I'm a way to ease the professional burden of the actual form tutor, who turns out has a lot going on right now. He introduced me to the group, oversaw chunks of some days, but on the whole I was 'left to it', so to speak, to become these students' form tutor. No targets; no discussions; no reflective process; nothing really to help me become a good form tutor – or even work out what a good form tutor looks like. In the school's defence, staff were always on hand if I sought them out for guidance, but it was very much 'my form' during that time.

Imagine if we took this approach to teacher training in general. Students left in the care of novices, with no formal approach to observations, target setting or development. Hopefully there would be uproar, and hopefully everyone would agree that 'yes, that seems like a terrible idea, I'm so glad that they changed it'.

So why is it that for so many teachers entering the system today, and who have been in the system for so long, that this approach to form tutors is so common? In the planning stages of this book back in March 2023 the editors surveyed educators through an online poll and over 70% of responses said that they received zero training on being a form tutor. All in all, 94.5% of all respondents said that in their teacher training they either had 'no training' or 'some, but it wasn't enough'.

DOI: 10.4324/9781003620976-1

The aim of this book is to address the paradox of what staff are told set against what staff are given. Staff are told everywhere that form tutors are 'the most important people in the school', 'the first line of safeguarding', 'first point of contact' etc. Ok, good – they should be. But where's the support to develop professional educators as professional form tutors?

The hope is that this book starts to do that, by offering readers a thorough and practical guide to professionals who are, who want to be, or want to develop, outstanding form tutors. This book will be about supporting professionals to be the best form tutors that they can be. Some professionals will want support with specific parts of the role – others may want broader support. Professionals in a leadership, training or mentoring capacity can use the book to offer training. Others may want to simply expand their repertoire. Use this book however it will help you the most.

Each chapter will focus on a particular strand of the role of a form tutor. Some will focus on how the role changes and will need to be adapted based on the age of the group (or clusters of students, if you are involved in vertical tutoring); some chapters will focus on external factors such as safeguarding and working with others; and some chapters will focus on internal strategies such as culture and ethos. Parts of the role are interconnected, so it would be worth remembering not to use chapters in complete isolation. For the sake of clarity, we'll be using the terms 'students', 'young people', 'pupils' pretty much interchangeably to help reflect the tone of the contributors. Similarly, the use of 'form time' and 'tutor time' may be used interchangeably based on the experiences of the contributors. Lastly, the book is aimed mostly at mainstream secondary schools, but we do hope that some of the skills and suggestions mentioned are transferable to other settings. The contributors will talk about 'Years' and 'Key Stages' as part of the English education system, but for any educators across the UK:

- Key Stage 3: Comprising of Years 7, 8 and 9 (England and Wales), Years 8, 9 and 10 (Northern Ireland) is generally comparable to Years S1, S2 and S3 (Scotland)
- Key Stage 4: C omprising of Years 10 and 11 (England and Wales), Years 11 and 12 (Northern Ireland) is generally comparable to S4 (Scotland)

- Key Stage 5: C omprising of Years 12 and 13 (England and Wales), Years 13 and 14 (Northern Ireland) is generally comparable to Years S5 and S6 (Scotland)

Whilst contributors will talk about 'GCSEs' as part of the English education system, all students undertaking any public examination will feel similar pressures, so please adapt accordingly to match your professional setting.

But first the nuts and bolts of the role. How can someone be a form tutor? Or become a better form tutor than they are already? Dozens of books, blogs, and sites can give you activities to do with your form – okay, but that makes me a quizmaster or a facilitator, not necessarily a tutor. We're not here to set quizzes, or to tell you the best ice breakers on a September morning. A few dozen more sites or articles will say 'it's all about positive relationships' but never really tell you how exactly these are forged. So to address this, and to get people actually thinking 'yes this is HOW to be a form tutor', I created a system known as **The 6Rs**;

- Relationships
- Rigour
- Reliable
- Rewards
- Receptive
- Routines

These are not to be used in isolation. Indeed in a wonderful metaphor for a successful form group, they work much better when being used together. So let's have a quick look at these before anything else.

Relationships

This is a word you'll probably notice being used a lot – the idea that positive relationships can lead to better outcomes has been explained by Sandilos and Rimm-Kaufman (2016). They in turn cite several works explaining how best – and how not to – form positive relationships with your students. Unsurprisingly, getting to know students' personalities; their interests; and spending time with them on an individual basis are shown to greatly improve student– teacher relationships. On a day-to-day basis this will resemble circulating around the class, offering mini-check-ins, asking questions about weekends, holidays, pets, etc. and remembering these to come back to them later down the road. The quality and clarity of communication can really benefit this relationship, as not only can it increase levels of trust, but also foster that positive and engaging classroom environment that is so important. Say what needs to be said, but do consider the best way to say it – is it a quiet conversation or addressing something in front of the group? Don't let a tutee walk away from a conversation unsure as to the purpose and outcome of that conversation.

Relationship-building absolutely takes time. You may win over one student one day, but a whole class may take months, maybe longer. If you find yourself, like I did, becoming a group's third successive tutor in as many years, it was only until the second school year did connections really form. A younger form, however, may be a quicker turnaround – the context behind the relationships is not to be underestimated. A great example that was shared over social media that was especially good for younger groups – run off a list of their birthdays from the data platform of the school, and buy 30 cheap cards or 'birthday pencils' in September. Have them ready in your drawer and be sure to hand them out ahead of time.

I would also stress the importance – supported by both Rimm-Kaufman and Sandilos (2016) and Jones et al. (2013) – to illustrate the need that one cannot prioritise building relationships over other professional responsibilities. If staff are consistently sarcastic, shout at students or classes, or belittle colleagues or the school, then the outcome tends to be students adopting similar strategies – resulting in a negative climate for the class.

Routines

It is well established that routines help students – indeed Argyropulo-Palmer (2022) has collated and summarised much of the evidence so I don't have to. A form tutor should use routines so that:

- they can create 'social norms' which leads to a more positive classroom culture (Blakemore, 2018)
- they reduce stimuli for students which leads to greater engagement with the teacher

As Argyropulo-Palmer explains, both of these lead us to the same goal: Students being able and willing to pay more attention to the teacher. This would then lead to a more positive climate within the classroom, allowing for the tutor to create those positive relationships we talked about. There is no point in having chats about pets, weekends and jet-skis if students are not prepared to pay attention to you – remember we do not sacrifice other professional aspects.

For a tutor, there will be two sets of routines that you want to foster. The first is the daily routine, and the second is the weekly routine (this may be set out by a school's pastoral team, SMSC lead, Personal Development lead, etc.). Both sets of routines may be dedicated by circumstance. Entrances, for example, will differ if you are in a science lab where the students cannot enter without staff, or a history classroom where they could. Does the school want students to wait outside or inside? What day is assembly on? Work within the parameters of what you have, and ensure consistency in your actions and the school expectations where possible. This is what I developed when I had a Year 7 class in a history room – students were expected to be in the room before staff finished their morning briefing.

Here is an example of an entrance routine, for Year 7, in a standard teaching classroom:

- Students allowed into the classroom before the first bell
- Students stand up when I enter the room after morning briefing
- I stand at the front of the room to say good morning and to check uniform
- Students sit down
- Register is taken – standard response is 'Yes Sir [or Ma'm etc.]'
- Notices given and questions answered
- Activity starts

Example of a weekly programme, set out by my Pastoral Lead:

Monday	Signing planners and checking in with the form
Tuesday	Assembly
Wednesday	Tutor a ctivity (I loved doing a Boggle, for instance)
Thursday	Newsround or current affairs
Friday	Silent reading or homework

This is pretty basic, but as the students and I were both new to the school – and the school allowed a fair amount of flexibility to their tutors – it worked for us (important note: Ensure routines work for all parties).

Rigour

When I was Head of Year, a number of my tutors were having a particularly hard time at building relationships with their groups. I met with them individually, and talked through what the issues were. And after a few questions and responses, the reasons became more and more evident:

Me	'Can we adapt the seating arrangement to benefit you more?'
Tutor	'Oh there isn't a seating plan, they sit where they want'.
Me	'Okay, so what have the parents said when you described their attitudes to form?'
Tutor	'Oh I haven't spoken to them, you're the first person I've told'.
Me	'Would you have a seating plan and contact home for a Year 10 class?'
Tutor	'Yes, why?'

There are lots of educationalists who connect 'rigour' with strictness – again, depending on your environment, this may or may not be the case. For me, however, I associate 'rigour' with the act of being thorough and with careful planning; that's how I intended to use it here.

The examples above highlight a lack of rigour: Form times were not thought out, they were not carefully considered, and as a result the outcomes were poor. Luckily, the professionals I had those conversations with were amongst the most positive, most coachable professionals I've had the pleasure to manage and were happy to address the issues as a team.

Too often from my experience, too many problems from form times originate from the idea that form time is secondary to lessons. It isn't planned as well, isn't monitored as much and isn't thought out. If we consider the elements of the **6Rs** – noticeably **routines** and **reliable** – then you'll really start to appreciate the need to be thoughtful with our **rigour**. My strongest piece of advice will be to apply the same **rigour** that you have for your lessons as you do for your form time – treat form time like a lesson and reap the benefits.

Reliable

You will have noticed by now (hopefully) that the **6Rs** work well when used collectively, collaboratively and consistently.

Some of you may be thinking that that last word, *consistently*, is a better fit. But let me tell you what I mean by being **reliable**. Yes, it has a strong element of being consistent, and yes, being consistent is massively helpful to you and your tutees. There is no point in carefully thought out tutor time on the Monday whilst you smile rainbows as you enforce **routines**, then an impromptu unplanned mess on the Tuesday with you being a grumpysaurus and letting everything slip by. Doesn't help you. Doesn't help them. But any dictionary definition of 'reliable' also denotes the need for *trustworthiness*. As in, can you, as a tutor, show that you can be trusted?

Niedlich et al. (2020) offer a comprehensive analysis of the role of trust in education, and find that high levels of trust from students increases academic achievement, student buy-in, and collective decision making – essentially a form group collaborating successfully.

Students who see teachers as reliable – as trustworthy – will buy into what those teachers are trying to achieve. Routines, culture and ethos, understanding that they are there to help them.

As a form tutor you will be privy to these students' lives and you may face safeguarding disclosures at some point. If the students trust you – if you are reliable in manner and action – they will want your help with things. If you are unreliable, they won't. As a form tutor you are the first line of pastoral welfare, and if students are not willing to approach you because you are seen as unreliable, you have compromised the welfare of those students. That's why there is a chapter dedicated to wellbeing and safeguarding in this book.

To be reliable you must be everything the dictionary says it is. You must be consistent. You must be trustworthy. You must be dependable. Do not confuse trustworthiness or reliability with being liked – part of this will mean that you follow through with consequences, with conversations, with anything. The 'consistency' translates to both your professional duties and your school policies.

Rewards

One of the brightest aspects of having a tutor group is really knowing these students – the relationships will take care of that, especially if you are the tutor for multiple years. Their favourite subjects, the obstacles that they may be going through, the toils, tribulations, and triumphs. When you know your students, you are in a better place to know what constitutes a reward for them. When I say **rewards**, this covers a wide range of possibilities. Praising in front of the group, praising away from the group (very important to distinguish which student would benefit from each approach there), certificates, emails or calls home, reward points as part of a school system – you should have an arsenal brimming with positivity.

Hopefully, the school in which you work has a behaviour and **rewards** system that is fit for purpose. **Rewards** policies are notoriously difficult. Often they need to be simple enough for Year 7s to understand and access it, but meticulous enough to include disenfranchised and older students that would rather not. So it is difficult, and school leaders have my utmost sympathy in trying to figure out this gordian knot. Rose (2016) wrote fabulously on the types of reward that we can offer students and picked apart various ideas and systems. In short, Rose explains that there is difficulty in having a consistent approach that maintains student interest. In a 'token economy', where X behaviour results in Y reward, how can we be sure that that behaviour is fairly assessed across a room full of students? He references Willingham (2005), suggesting that students – unlike when dealing with poor behaviour – respond well when praise and rewards are slightly unpredictable. Overall though, it is believed that reinforcement through **rewards** can work better than punishment.

So how does this translate into your form room?

Well, for the 'token economy' approach, it can be as simple as a merit for every uniform check, equipment check, and signed planner that a student presents. They'll know the score beforehand, and know the reward is coming. Remember the **reliable** part of the **6Rs**?

The unpredictability element could be positive emails to home for attitude, improvement, showing community spirit, anything really. Too often schools communicate either information or bad news, so short emails can go a long way.

And for reinforcement? Find the kids who do the little things right, all of the time, and don't forget them. Maybe pastoral teams will do end-of-term awards? Or a positive comment on a Monday morning to that student? Remember a reward doesn't have to be a physical item per se, but be relentless in positive reinforcement, the support and the praise.

Receptive

One of my favourite things about being a form tutor is that every single form group is like its own small community. There are quirky characters, dramatic characters, switched on characters. There are cliques. There are personalities. And above all, there is a group dynamic, a collective persona.

My last point here – and the last of the **6Rs** – is that in order to make the most out of your tutor group, is to be as **receptive** as you can to all of it. Be welcoming, be interested in the quirks and the personalities; and to your role in harnessing it. The students often make the form, and you are there to lead and to guide them. Encourage the energetic students to become leaders, the quieter students to be contributors, to offer strategies to the students who may have more obstacles than others. Be **receptive** to them, embrace the personalities and personality of the group, and then utilise it to yours and the group's advantage.

However, your role will also very much refer to the need to be **receptive** to the context of the group. If you have a group for several years, the dynamics and stresses of students will inevitably change over time. Students may come into and out of the group. Exam and relationship pressures will impact Key Stage 4 more than Key Stage 3.

As you read through this book, be **receptive** to how you can evolve or revolutionise your role as a form tutor. For each chapter, think back to these **6Rs** and you'll see a continuing theme of how to use these concepts. The **rigour** of safeguarding and attendance; the **relationships** between key adults; the need to be **reliable** and use **routines** and **rewards** across all key stages and how they will change over time. In short, use these **6Rs** – and this book – to be the best tutor that you can be: **An outstanding form tutor.**

References and Bibliography

Argyropulo-Palmer, A.-M. (2025) *Exploring the evidence base: The role of routines in creating an effective learning environment.* Available at https://my.chartered.college/impact_article/exploring-the-evidence-base-the-role-of-routines-in-creating-an-effective-learning-environment/ (Accessed 26 January 2026).

Blakemore, S. J. (2018) 'Avoiding social risk in adolescence', *Current Directions in Psychological Science*, 27(2), pp. 116–122. Available at https://psycnet.apa.org/record/2018-14983-009 (Accessed 26 January 2026).

Jones, S., Bouffard, S. and Weissbourd, R. (2013) *Educators' social and emotional skills vital to learning.* Available at https://www.nationalresilienceresource.com/Education/Educators_social_and_emotional_skills.pdf (Accessed 26 January 2026).

Niedlich, S., Kallfass, A., Pohle, S. and Bormann, I. (2021) 'A comprehensive view of trust in education: Conclusions from a systematic literature review', *Review of Education*, 9(1), pp. 124–158. Available at https://doi.org/10.1002/rev3.3239 (Accessed 26 January 2026).

Rose, N. (2016) *The psychology of behaviour management (part 1).* Available at https://evidenceintopractice.wordpress.com/2016/01/10/the-psychology-of-behaviour-management-part-1/ (Accessed 26 January 2026).

Sandilos, L. E., Rimm-Kaufman, S. E. and Cohen, J. J. (2016) 'Warmth and demand: The relation between students' perceptions of the classroom environment and achievement growth', *Child Development*, 88(4), pp. 1321–1337. Available at https://doi.org/10.1111/cdev.12685 (Accessed 26 January 2026).

Willingham, D. T. (2005) *Ask the cognitive scientist: How praise can motivate – or stifle.* Available at https://www.aft.org/ae/winter2005-2006/willingham (Accessed 26 January 2026).

1 Knowing Your Form

The Foundation of Relational Education

Mark McKie

The discussion emphasises a strategic approach centered on the **'6Rs'** – particularly **reliable**, **receptive**, and **routines** – to build a 'low-threat' environment. Ultimately, I believe that the tutor–student bond is a vital safety net, advocating for a holistic, asset-based partnership between school and home to ensure every young person feels seen, respected and supported.

Why? The Foundational Imperative of Connection and Care

The shift from childhood to adolescence, often marked by the transition into secondary school, represents a period of profound vulnerability (Bagnall et al., 2021). It is during this time that students, grappling with burgeoning identities and new social pressures, most urgently require stability, validation, and a sense of belonging. The reasons why form tutors must prioritise 'knowing their form' are deeply rooted in addressing these complex student needs, thereby creating an environment where learning across all lessons can occur largely unobstructed by anxiety or alienation.

The learning ecosystem of a young person is a triangle involving the student, the school, and the home. As will be explained in Chapter 7: Working With Others, a positive relationship with home is very important to ensure that there is a shift from deficit communication, which focuses on problematic behaviöurs (ThinkForward, 2024), to an asset-based partnership that mobilises a student's internal resources to address the underlying trauma (Ebersöhn and Eloff,

DOI: 10.4324/9781003620976-2

2006). Having a good relationship with families increases the willingness to share important information about the young person. By viewing parents and carers not as external observers but as co-educators with invaluable insight, the form tutor will gain lots of helpful information and viewpoints about their students.

Getting to know your form group is an amazing journey of discovery, where carefully considered interactions and sharing of personal information will provide the fullest possible picture of each student outside the academic environment. This picture is vital for smoothing the journey through early adolescence and academic studies. Disclosure of personal information by the form tutor is a personal choice, but I have found that sharing information about myself encourages more openness in reply from students, which reveals a more detailed picture. My form groups all know my age, favourite music, foods, sports and opinions on things that interest young people such as social media, tattoos and piercings. Using these pieces of information as conversation starters is safe and I show myself as accepting of other opinions, but demonstrate that I or they do not have to change our opinions. Alongside these snippets of shared information lies a need to safeguard the form tutor: I make sure that I know, understand and follow professional standards and school policies on social media. I do not disclose addresses or any information that could be deemed inappropriate to share with young people.

Being in the job for over 30 years up to this point, I have worked with five tutor groups from Years 7–11 and sixth-form groups. I have worked with less experienced teachers to develop their skillset as a form tutor. Just like our favourite soap operas, in these multiple groups of young people I have seen many stereotypes appear. Whilst any observer of people will find it easy to spot these stereotypes, the understanding of the reasons behind this presentation first thing in the day is much more complex. I have considered many of the young people I have grown to know so well and combined many into one fictional character that any form tutor is likely to find in their precious form group.

Young People With Education System Labels

At the start of every new school year teachers are bombarded with data about students. Somewhere in this pile of numbers, flags and coloured boxes on spreadsheets will be data about their tutor group. A quality form tutor must master the 'school-provided labels' – the official classifications used to identify students who are systematically vulnerable or require statutory support. These designations, the main ones being Special Educational Needs and Disabilities (SEND), Pupil Premium (PP) and Looked After Children (LAC) – are vital data points that require targeted resource allocation and instructional adjustments across the curriculum. It is around these students that a form tutor will need to provide the most advocacy, reassurance and reliability and can make the most difference to life chances.

Such labels follow students through their school life and students will require differing amounts of support at different times. I have found that transition years require close monitoring, but also, making choices such as GCSE options and preparing for assessments can cause heightened anxiety related to understanding processes and self-esteem.

I met Freddy as he started Year 7. He was a SEND student with strong autistic traits that were focussed on sensations caused by touch. He struggled with standard uniform materials and adaptations were made to ease his discomfort. He would also become distressed if touched by anybody else – a challenging problem in a busy school environment. Early transition passes helped keep Freddy away from crowds but I had a bigger effect on him. Every day I would play rock-paper-scissors with Freddy. Gradually I offered a high-five reward which Freddy accepted. Four years on and Freddy still wants to play rock-paper-scissors and we enjoy high-five hand contact.

The Anxious One

These guys are easy to spot in the form. Indicators include withdrawal, constant checking of information and overload of preparedness. Harry transitioned to secondary as an academically high-achieving young man. The first day I saw him he was carrying a backpack that looked large enough for a week in the Lake District. During my daily round of conversations I had a chat with him. He had brought literally everything he could possibly need for school. I pointed out that he only needed his PE kit on certain days. Other equipment and books would also only be needed on days dictated by his timetable. Although most students respond to this type of help, Harry did not change and continued to bring his mega-bag daily, all through Year 7 and into Year 8. This behaviour, along with others, was communicated between school professionals and eventually led to Harry being assessed for Autism Spectrum Disorder (ASD). Following a diagnosis, support mechanisms were triggered across school that helped Harry return to his academic success.

Julia needed her timetable explaining every day for the first half term or so, but then became less anxious about being in the wrong place. I would take the register, then straight away sit with her to make sure that she knew what lesson was at which point in the day and the location. As time went on she needed less support, until in Years 10 and 11 when formal examination timetables appeared. I was ready to support her, knowing already what support she needed.

At the start of Year 7 there are many anxious students, but as time goes on the number will usually reduce. Research states that the educational landscape is marked by an undeniable rise in school-related anxiety among young people (NHS England, 2023). This is not merely a transient nervousness but often manifests as clinically significant emotional distress that severely impacts attendance, engagement and performance. Students entering secondary education face an immediate escalation of expectations: Greater academic rigour, a more complex schedule involving multiple teachers, a larger and less familiar physical environment and a more challenging social hierarchy.

Anxiety fundamentally interferes with the brain's ability to process and retain information. When a student is in a state of hyper-arousal, the prefrontal cortex – the area responsible for executive functions like planning, reasoning and working memory – is effectively hijacked by the amygdala, the brain's emotional centre. A form tutor who 'knows their form' is highly attuned to the subtle, and often silent, indicators of this internal struggle. By proactively understanding the emotional baseline and triggers of each student, the form tutor can move from reactive discipline or instruction to proactive support. I regularly explain anxieties to teaching colleagues, share information with pastoral colleagues and maintain regular conversations with parents and carers to ensure that as much helpful support as possible is put into place. My target is to create a predictable, compassionate, and low-threat classroom environment where the need for acceptance and belonging is met before the need for academic performance is imposed.

The Protestor/Rebel

It is simply part of growing up and developing that young people will at times be a little difficult or challenging. Rebellion against rules in young people is a complex psycho-social phenomenon, often stemming from the essential developmental task of establishing an independent identity (Erikson, 1968). As adolescents transition from childhood dependence, they increasingly challenge rules and authority as a means of testing boundaries and asserting autonomy, a drive that often intensifies when they perceive rules as arbitrary, unfair, or restrictive of their personal freedom. Schools (especially in England) seem to be full of rules that fit these criteria. Most young people will quietly whine about the rules but some young people can take this to another level, however, and you will not need a quiet conversation to hear or see their protest.

Faye started her protest stage early in Year 8. She started to wear makeup which gradually became denser upon her face. Her skirt seemed to shrink daily, both of which were in direct defiance of school rules. When spoken to, a conversation that took many revisits, Faye explained that she was 'between friendship groups' and was struggling to fit in with anyone. Faye had adopted her rebellious behaviours to gain status or acceptance within her peer group. Fortunately for both, Faye had a repeatedly positive relationship with me, which made the conversation easier. Faye believed that I had her best interests in mind so an agreement was struck to reduce the layers of makeup and lower the skirt to a length that would keep within the rules. Constant checking and reminding was needed, but Faye did fit into her new friendship group.

George struggled to keep himself quiet in school. He seemed angry about everything he was ever asked to do. Demonstrating to him that I would be an advocate for him by speaking on his behalf to teachers, we built what was initially a tentative but overall positive relationship that was broken and rebuilt many times.

Amelia seemed to have a hand that spent more time in the air than at her side. It seemed that every time I gave the group a gentle reminder of a school rule up it flew. 'But Sir, what effect does X have on my learning?', where X could include: Makeup, wearing a coat in lesson, hair colour, footwear, skirt length, school ties, jewellery – amongst many others – and 'Y is against my human rights', where Y could include: Not going to the toilet during lesson time, long lunch queues, staying in designated student areas at break. Amelia listened closely to every attempted reason I gave for these dictates and then replied with opposing arguments. Encouraging her to participate in student leadership gave her the opportunity to take these arguments to a forum which could effect change.

Of course the reasons behind such rebelliousness can be hiding other serious situations. Special Educational Needs and Disabilities (SEND), Looked After Children (LAC) and Pupil Premium (PP) students often use rebellion to mask their underlying traumas, most of which are too great for an adolescent mind to deal with. According to Bomber (2007) rebellion is not a character flaw, but a neurological adaptation to an unsafe world. In adolescents who have faced significant trauma, the brain stem (survival) and limbic system (emotions) are over-developed, while the prefrontal cortex (executive function) remains underdeveloped or 'offline'.

The Late Again Student

Persistent lateness is a potential indicator of many situations. It is something that can happen in regular daily bouts, over the occasional few days or patterned days over time. Conversations with the student or parents will often reveal the cause, some of which will require a little bending of the school expectations.

Sam was a really nice young man, so polite and hard working. He started to be late to school several days a week – not much, just 10–15 minutes. Sam was a PP student, but this is not hugely relevant at this time. The school policy was that Sam would be given detentions for his lateness, which I explained to him. 'Fair enough', he replied. I spoke with him about how things were in the morning in his house. It eventually came to light that his mum had found a new job which started before school. This meant that Sam was left in charge of getting his two younger siblings out of bed, fed and to primary school, a struggle in itself. Then he had to get himself to secondary school. Given Sam's age, his caring responsibilities were considered appropriate, and with the agreement of the Year Leader, some flexibility was allowed regarding his lateness.

Young carers undertake significant caring responsibilities for a family member. These students frequently arrive having already completed a set of adult-level tasks, and are profoundly stressed, preoccupied, and emotionally drained. The start of the day for a young carer is a forced separation from their primary responsibilities. 'Knowing your form' means establishing an environment of confidential, immediate safety. The form tutor must guard against the assumption that a young carer's occasional failure to meet homework deadlines is laziness; rather, it is a consequence of competing and urgent domestic demands, requiring differentiated deadline management. There will probably be other professionals in school whose role is to monitor young carers. Chapter 3: Attendance and Punctuality contains more guidance on this issue.

The Sporting Success

The commitment required of high-achieving young sports people often means their school day begins long before the first bell with gruelling training sessions. Lucy was a swimmer competing in national standard competitions. Swimming seems to be the most demanding of training regimes as it is one of few where the athlete often trains twice in a day. This dedication presents a unique educational challenge: Lucy arrived many days physically depleted and mentally exhausted. For me as her form teacher, 'knowing your form' meant understanding Lucy's training load and schedule. This awareness allowed my role to shift from demanding alertness to offering compassionate flexibility. She was allowed to 'zone out' for a while during time used by me to check in and mentor individuals, during which time she sorted her hair out and ate a second breakfast in the classroom. Recognising this hidden curriculum of fatigue ensures the student is not penalised for commitments that are otherwise supported by the school community, a key aspect of holistic student support. Discussions with her parents ensured that I could advocate for her in the most helpful ways. In Lucy's case it was explaining to teachers that her homework would be late when due immediately after competition weekends unless enough time was given beforehand.

The Forgetful One

Sean was a great attender, very polite and a wonderful story teller. He did, however, seem to have a memory like a sieve. Every day (or so it appeared) Sean would wait patiently for me to ask him, 'So what have you forgotten today Sean?' His answers would vary from pieces of homework, PE kit, pencil case, forgetting to charge his Chromebook and on some special days his tie. When Sean was asked about these ongoing problems he explained how his life was split between his parents' houses, and the things that he needed each day always seemed to be at the wrong house. Helping Sean to make a timetable for his homes did help him remember to take the right things with him to the other parent. Sean (along with his parents) did learn to cope with his new life and he became more accountable for his organisation, but I always had spare equipment for him to use.

Students navigating shared parenting arrangements, particularly those with frequent transitions between homes, often face logistical and emotional hurdles that culminate in stress right at the school gate. Transitions can lead to a feeling of disorientation and practical problems like forgetting essential materials. For the form tutor, 'knowing your form' means being aware of the student's custody calendar and, crucially, involving reducing administrative penalties for logistical mishaps. This acknowledgment that their home life is inherently more complex validates the student's reality and reduces the conflicts of loyalty for a young person living between split families that can manifest as anxiety upon arrival.

The One Not in Uniform

Believe it or not a lot of young people like to be in uniform, There is a safety brought about by looking as one with their peers. Given this, why would any young person not be in uniform?

Laura stopped wearing the correct uniform. At first it was a sweatshirt that she refused to remove. Then came the leggings rather than a skirt. Of course, the leggings were worn with trainers as well. Referral to the pastoral team eventually revealed one of those very sad home life stories that still occur in our society today. Her outright defiance was a callout to be really noticed and helped. She was testing the system to see how much she really mattered to any adult as she felt that she did not matter much at home. She was using her behaviour to communicate her relational needs to adults in a non-verbal way as she found verbalising her needs far too distressing.

The Religiously Different One

Religious identity is a powerful, intrinsic component of a student's selfhood, yet it often represents an 'unseen curriculum' that significantly impacts their experience and engagement within a secular school environment. This requires a form tutor moving beyond mere religious tolerance to active, informed, and proactive inclusion.

Students belonging to minority religious groups frequently navigate a school environment where the prevailing cultural norms may not reflect their home life, leading to feelings of alienation or invisibility. The teacher's role is not simply to just accept these differences but to foster an environment of celebration and recognition. This involves ensuring that school activities, dietary provisions, and clothing policies are not only compliant with policy but are actively and respectfully facilitated. Celebrating the diversity of religious festivals sends a powerful signal of belonging and validation to students whose identities are often marginalised, enhancing their sense of psychological safety.

Effective support for students with diverse faith commitments is impossible without the form tutor increasing their personal knowledge regarding the student's specific belief system and practices. Ali was a Muslim student, one of very few in the school. He did not seek out special recognition, but very much enjoyed quietly explaining the reasons behind his religion's holy days and festivals. The simple act of listening and showing genuine interest in a core pillar of Ali's life encouraged other students to participate in the conversation. As I am not religious, I initially felt unqualified to discuss religion, but Ali showed me that conversations about religious activities can be as normal as talking about football results.

The One That Makes the Choice to...

Whilst I have illustrated a range of young people with 'back stories' and reasons for their presentation at the start of the day, there is always the chance that the behaviour is just a choice.

Alfie chose to be late every lesson. He arrived at school in plenty of time, he simply liked to be with his friends as much as possible.

Beth struggled to complete homework. She had no reason, she just chose to try to avoid doing work outside of school.

Stella arrived every day with her tie in her bag. She left me wearing it, but I could guarantee that it would be missing before the first lesson.

All of these young people needed clear lines to be drawn and school policies to be followed. Appropriate sanctions and support processes did resolve some, but not all choices. Some young people just choose to be 'in trouble' throughout their school life. I have always found this to be the hardest pill to swallow, but in truth this does not mean I have failed as a tutor.

I cannot count how many pupils I greet every day with a short skirt, white socks, top buttons undone, shirts not tucked in, blazer not worn, earrings, etc. etc. Every day is the same mini-battle. The message is constant: 'I care and I will correct you nicely so that you do not have conflict with other staff later in the day'. It will be tiring, frustrating and so, so repetitive, but each little win accumulates and these are what you must focus on.

For some young people, the relationship with their form tutor will be the strongest relationship with any adult in the school. Nurture these and enjoy every moment.

- Remember and implement the **6Rs.**
- Greet at the door. Watch every face as they come in. Correct small things now. 'Shirt in please!'
- Once the formal parts of your form time are complete, get amongst your young people. Have conversations that others can join in or hear at their level in the student space.
- Check in with vulnerable students every day.
- Every day is a new day. Believe that a relationship damaged yesterday will be rebuilt today.

References and Bibliography

Bagnall, C., Skipper, Y. and Fox, C. (2019) '"You're in this world now": Students', teachers' and parents' experiences of school transition and how they feel it can be improved, *British Journal of Educational Psychology*, 90(1), pp. 206–226. Available at https://bpspsychub.onlinelibrary.wiley.com/doi/10.1111/bjep.12273 (Accessed 31 January 2026).

Bombèr, L. (2007) *Inside i'm hurting: Practical strategies for supporting children with attachment difficulties in schools.* Worth Publishing.
Ebersöhn, L. and Eloff, I. (2006) *Life skills and assets.* 2nd edition. Van Schaik.
Erikson, E. H. (1968) *Identity: youth and crisis.* W. W. Norton.
NHS England (2023) *Mental health of children and young people in England, 2023: Wave 4 follow up to the 2017 survey.* Available at https://digital.nhs.uk/data-and-information/publications/statistical/mental-health-of-children-and-young-people-in-england/2023-wave-4-follow-up (Accessed 18 January 2026).
ThinkForward (2024). *Asset-based guide.* Available at https://thinkforward.org.uk/asset-based-guide/ (Accessed 16 January 2026).

2 Wellbeing and Safeguarding

Olivia Saunders

Introduction

When we think about the role of a form tutor, it makes sense to begin with the young people themselves. Every student who sits in front of you is at a particular stage of development, and as a tutor it is vital to understand what this means in practice. The adolescent brain is not simply a smaller version of the adult brain; it is a highly impressionable and rapidly developing system. Understanding how it works equips tutors with the insight needed to adapt their practice, respond to challenges with empathy, and create environments that support healthy development and learning.

Within this context, safeguarding and wellbeing are not separate responsibilities but integral to the day-to-day role of the form tutor. Safeguarding can be understood as the actions taken to protect students from harm and to promote their welfare, while wellbeing refers to a student's emotional, psychological, and physical state, and their ability to engage successfully with learning. A secure understanding of adolescent development enables tutors to recognise when behaviour may be a communication of unmet need, distress, or risk, rather than a deliberate choice to misbehave. Informed by this understanding, tutors are better equipped to respond with empathy, adapt their practice, and create an environment where students feel safe, supported, and able to reach their potential.

Supporting Adolescent Brain Development

A headteacher I once worked with described some of our most vulnerable students as 'chaos navigators', moving through households marked

DOI: 10.4324/9781003620976-3

by uncertainty, conflict and unpredictability. Against this backdrop, the role of the form tutor is to provide a reliable touchpoint: A consistent and safe space that supports students' physical and emotional development.

Within any tutor group there will be students with a wide range of lived experiences, yet all share the same fundamental need for secure attachment. Bowlby's attachment theory suggests that children are biologically driven to seek proximity to a caregiver, with secure attachment formed through consistent and responsive care (Bowlby, 1969). When this need is not met, research indicates that brain development can be affected, particularly in relation to emotional regulation and decision making.

Educational psychologist Jaak Panksepp emphasises the importance of safe and emotionally supportive environments for effective learning and sound decision-making (Panksepp, 2004). For students who have experienced trauma or neglect, difficulties with executive functioning may emerge, increasing the likelihood of impulsive or emotionally driven behaviour in the classroom.

So what does this mean for you as a form tutor? It is likely that at least one student in your group will present with an insecure attachment style shaped by early experiences of inconsistency or neglect. This may influence their ability to self-regulate, manage emotions and make considered choices. In this context, the tutor's role becomes a safeguarding and wellbeing function, offering consistency, stability, and emotional safety within the tutor group.

Tutor time often includes elements of PSHE or character development, and when delivered intentionally, these sessions provide valuable opportunities to explicitly teach self-regulation strategies and support students' wellbeing. Over time, a warm, welcoming and predictable tutor environment may also position you as a trusted adult that a student feels safe enough to approach. This may involve helping them reflect on their behaviour or creating space for them to share their experiences.

It is important to be clear that the role of the form tutor is not to fix the difficulties a student may disclose. That responsibility sits with the school's safeguarding team and wider support systems. However, what we do know is that developing brains are profoundly shaped by experience and for some students, the consistency and care offered during tutor time may represent one of the most protective factors in their school day.

With that in mind, when stepping into the role of form tutor, it is worth reflecting on the following:

1. What will be the same every day when student X walks into my classroom? Simple **routines** can give students a sense of stability. Consider what needs to be the same every time a student walks into your classroom, such as a daily greeting at the door, a clear place for belongings, or a short check-in task on the board. These all send the message: *You are seen, you are safe, and you belong here.*
2. What is the climate I want to create within my tutor room? Think about how you want students to think and feel when they are in your classroom. Should they be excited and inquisitive or calm and reflective? Consider what you need to do to set the correct tone. Think about how you use your voice, manage transitions, or celebrate success.
3. How will I create that climate, and what visible artefacts will student X encounter every time they step into this space? Relational **routines** help create a sense of belonging. A consistent seating plan, regular reflection questions, brief 1:1 check-ins, and celebrating effort all help students feel settled, noticed, and valued in the space. Language as an environmental artefact shapes the climate. Using names confidently, offering calm correction, separating behaviour from the child, and reassuring students they will be taken seriously – all contribute to a safe space.

Supporting Physical and Mental Health Needs

In today's society, it is essential that students understand that we all have mental health, and that there are actions we can take to support positive mental health. Within most schools there will be a tutor-time curriculum that tutors are expected to deliver. While these vary in content, length and rigour, they typically cover themes of personal development. This provides tutors with a valuable opportunity to help young people recognise and respond to their own physical and mental health needs. Tutors play a fundamental role in ensuring students develop both a sense of self and an awareness of their wellbeing.

In my previous role, I worked with tutors to upskill them in noticing early signs of concern; for example, a student appearing unusually sleepy, or another struggling with personal hygiene. Insights like these were then shared with the Head of Year, and when themes occurred, the tutor-time schedule could be adapted: Tutors were provided with sessions responsive to student needs. In this way, the pastoral team was able to shape the curriculum, so it was truly responsive to the cohort. This kind of best practice would not have been possible without the insight and vigilance of form tutors.

As a tutor, it is important to remain alert to the specific needs of the cohort in front of you. The best tutors are flexible and adapt their sessions to meet the challenges their students face. While 20–30 minutes of tutor time can feel brief, small, focused activities can make a significant difference. Below are some scenarios and suggested responses. If your school covers Personal Development topics using dedicated curriculum time (usually called PSHE, Life Skills or Personal Development), these scenarios and responses are just as as viable for you as a tutor to look out for specific health needs of your tutees:

Physical Health Need

Observation: You notice that many students in your tutor group are drinking energy drinks and eating sweets before school.

Action: Plan a short, responsive session on the importance of a balanced diet. Use platforms such as PSHE Association or Twinkl for resources, or as stated in Chapter 7: Working With Others, consult with your wider pastoral team to see if any colleagues have deployed successful strategies. Revisit the theme later in the term, inviting students to share changes they have made. This could even become a tutor group challenge, with recognition or rewards for those who make the biggest positive changes.

Mental Health Need

Observation: As assessment week approaches, a large number of students appear anxious about exams and unsure how to prepare.

Action: Facilitate a discussion around what worry feels like, normalising it as a shared emotion. Follow this up with simple strategies such as building positive routines, using motivational statements or affirmations, or adopting healthy study habits. Even a short activity like this can have a significant impact. Where there is flexibility in the timetable, you could extend the session to include practical study skills, equipping students with tools to manage anxiety more effectively.

For both examples, it is recommended that any concerns are uploaded onto your school's safeguarding system and communicated to the wider pastoral staff.

It is important to acknowledge that many of the factors contributing to a young person's physical and mental health lie outside of your control. However, by creating a consistent environment with clear **routines**, responding to needs as they arise, and embedding education around positive habits, you can play a pivotal role in helping students thrive at school.

Positive, Not Punitive

Creating a culture of reward is key to establishing a successful tutor environment. B. F. Skinner's Behaviour Theory, developed across the 1930s–1950s, suggests that positive reinforcement strengthens desired behaviours (Skinner, 1965). A successful form tutor will embed positive reinforcement as part of tutor time culture. Publicly praising tutees strengthens **relationships**, builds confidence, and contributes to student wellbeing. It also provides a foundation from which you can challenge undesirable behaviours when they arise. This approach can be particularly powerful in securing student success in areas of school life that may otherwise prove difficult. For example, a form tutor who routinely acknowledges kindness and co-operation can shape group norms and reduce conflict between students. Similarly, a tutor who consistently recognises punctuality, effort, organisation, or positive peer interactions during morning registration may see improved attendance, greater engagement in tutor activities, and more settled behaviour across the group. Students who feel noticed for doing the right thing are often more willing to accept redirection when expectations are not met, as **relationships** are grounded in trust rather than correction.

When starting out as a tutor, it is worth dedicating time to consider how you will recognise and celebrate student success within tutor time. In doing this, you should be mindful of whole-school **rewards** systems and think carefully about how what you offer within your tutor time can complement existing systems and procedures. What is especially effective is when your personality as a practitioner shines through in your choice of recognition.

In one school I worked in, a colleague introduced a creative reward system using themed 'reward slips' that reflected the time of year. For example, during the final weeks of the summer term students could receive 'Sunshine Slips' for demonstrating positive behaviours such as helping a peer or supporting a teacher. By focusing on non-academic behaviours, this system engaged students well and promoted a culture of positive relationships, emphasising the importance of community and mutual support, both of which are essential to a healthy tutor group culture. The strategic placement of slips being awarded at the end of term also gave students extra motivation at a time which could be most challenging due to fatigue. This was something that my colleague recognised his students needed.

It is important to acknowledge that creating a positive culture does not mean ignoring occasions when students fall short of expectations. A key aspect of the tutor role is ensuring that students feel accountable to you. If you manage to establish this sense of accountability, you can often prevent low-level issues from escalating to the Head of Year or senior staff. That said, it can feel challenging to address negative behaviour when you have worked hard to establish yourself as a student's champion.

A mantra that has served me well is "praise in public and reprimand in private". In practice, this can be challenging. If a student behaves inappropriately during a tutor time session, it can be tempting to address it immediately so the session can continue. For some students, this approach may work without issue. However, for others, dealing with the behaviour publicly can harm the relationship. It may cause feelings of shame or embarrassment.

A more effective strategy could be to approach the student privately. Briefly let them know their behaviour was not acceptable at their table or set the class off on an independent activity while inviting the student to discuss the matter quietly at the front. For students with more complex behaviour, it is often better to revisit the issue later at a separate time, outside of tutor time. This allows space for discussion and restorative work to take place. A way that you may address an issue later is by attending the student's next lesson and arranging a time to speak with the young person at another point during the day; for example having a follow- up chat at break time or after school. By reprimanding in private, and doing so in a supportive manner, you reduce the risk of judgement and criticism, preserve the relationship, and increase the likelihood of a positive response. This reinforces the importance of protecting a student's self-concept, even when addressing poor behaviour.

As a tutor, you are a young person's champion. In the words of Pierson (2013): 'Every child deserves a champion – an adult who will never give up on them, who understands the power of connection, and insists that they become the best that they can possibly be'.

Coaching Students to Improve

There are many facets to the role of a tutor, yet it could be argued that coaching is one of the most important. Supporting students to set goals, build self-regulation and develop resilience is not only crucial to their success in school, but also in life beyond the classroom. For many years, the emphasis has rested heavily on academic outcomes for young people. However, in the wake of the pandemic, and in the midst of a digital age filled with misinformation and uncertainty, building character has become just as important as academic achievement for future success.

Coaching can be a key driver of student growth. As a tutor, you are in a unique position: Through frequent touchpoints across the school week you can offer consistency, provide reinforcement and celebrate progress. You also have deeper insight into who your students are, which enables you to help them set meaningful goals and work on areas that may not always be visible to subject teachers.

Adopting a coaching mindset empowers students by encouraging them to develop their own solutions rather than being told what to do (Van Nieuwerburgh, 2012). This is particularly powerful because many students experience the teacher–student relationship as largely directive. By contrast, the tutor role allows you to step away from that dynamic, offering opportunities for active listening, questioning, and reflection in a non-judgemental space.

The demands of school life can be extensive and often call for a growth mindset. As Dweck (2006) suggests, helping students reframe challenges and setbacks as opportunities for growth can transform how they approach both learning and life. Tutor time, therefore, can serve as a vehicle to explicitly nurture values such as resilience, perseverance and self-belief, qualities that will sustain students well beyond their school years.

Creating an environment where students can think critically, share openly and explore solutions not only helps them address immediate challenges, but also builds character that contributes to greater success both in school and beyond.

Safeguarding Is Key

Keeping Children Safe in Education (KCSIE) states that 'safeguarding and promoting the welfare of children is everyone's responsibility' (Department for Education, 2025, p. 7). As a form tutor, you see your students every single day, placing you in a prime position to notice patterns, concerns and everyday changes, such as declining attendance, unusual tiredness, friendship breakdowns or shifts in mood. Any one of these factors could signal a deeper safeguarding concern. The earlier concerns are identified, the quicker interventions can be put in place to support the young person and prevent issues from escalating. All teachers should receive training across the course of the academic year in school safeguarding practices and things to look out for.

Seeing your tutees daily gives you an excellent opportunity to establish positive relationships, something explored in other chapters of this book. When it comes to safeguarding, these relationships are crucial if a student chooses to make a disclosure. Students are most likely to share concerns with staff they feel comfortable with. It is therefore vital that 'all staff should know what to do if a child tells them they are being abused, exploited, or neglected' (Department for Education, 2025, p. 9).

However, it is important to remember that as a form tutor you are not responsible for investigating or fixing the problem. Here is what you should do if a child shares a concern with you:

1. Stay calm, listen, and maintain composure
2. Validate and reassure the student that they have been heard
3. Communicate the next steps clearly and inform the Designated Safeguarding Lead (DSL)
4. Record the concern factually, including dates, times and specific information. Do not include your own interpretations
5. Prioritise the student's safety above all else.

Identifying patterns and reporting concerns is a major part of the tutor role. It is natural for this responsibility to feel daunting. To prepare yourself, ensure you understand the basics of safeguarding and know what it is that you need to look out for. Professional curiosity is key, as all children, regardless of background, can be at risk. Working closely with your school's DSL and safeguarding team is essential, but knowing the key areas of the latest version of KCSIE will strengthen your practice and confidence.

Tutors should be familiar with the four main types of abuse and common potential indicators:

1. *Physical Abuse*

- Unexplained injuries
- Unusual explanations for injuries
- Wearing inappropriate clothing

2. *Emotional Abuse*

- Overly anxious or fearful
- Reluctant to socialise
- Developmental delays without medical cause
- Over-compliance

3. *Sexual Abuse*

- Difficulty walking or sitting
- Frequent visits to the toilet
- Avoiding specific people
- Knowledge or behaviour that is not age- appropriate

4. *Neglect*

- Poor hygiene or appearance
- Inadequate clothing
- Unmet health needs
- Hunger and malnutrition
- Developmental concerns
- Getting into unsafe situations

Understanding these categories and the signs associated with each helps you notice concerns and respond appropriately.

Some signs can appear across all abuse areas, so it is helpful to remain alert to additional indicators, such as:

- Behavioural changes
- School absence
- Signs of secrecy
- Low self-esteem
- Risk-taking behaviours
- Reluctance to go home
- Mental health concerns
- Changes in physical presentation

This is not an exhaustive list, but being vigilant to these concerns will put you in a strong position to safeguard your students effectively. Recognising signs and responding appropriately ensures that students receive the support they need and demonstrates your genuine interest in their wellbeing. You are showing that you care about who they are, the challenges they face, and how you can support them to succeed.

These efforts often result in meaningful rewards, such as a heartfelt thank you after exam results, a calmer response in a behaviour incident, or a breakthrough in a subject where a student previously struggled. When these moments occur, they reinforce why your role matters and highlight the profound impact of attentive, committed tutoring.

To summarise: When you build strong relationships and establish consistent habits and routines, you provide your tutees with both security and stability. This not only creates an environment where they feel safe and able to flourish, but also enables you to notice changes, address concerns, and offer the steady support they need. Safeguarding young people is always high stakes, but a powerful starting point is to create a space where they feel cared for, heard and equipped with the tools to manage their own wellbeing with confidence. Alongside school policies and the guidance of the Designated Safeguarding Lead, form tutors can further strengthen their practice by drawing on trusted national resources such as NSPCC Learning, Keeping Children Safe in Education; the UK Safer Internet Centre; and the Anna Freud Centre, which provide clear, up-to-date guidance to support both safeguarding and wellbeing.

- Build a regular routine into tutor time that allows students to reflect on challenges or setbacks and to think intentionally about how they might overcome them. This reflection could take place weekly, monthly, or even once per half-term. Giving students this space provides you with valuable insight into their struggles and enables you to use tutor time as a tool for responsive support.
- Read the latest version of Keeping Children Safe in Education (KCSIE) and consider what this means practically for your role as form tutor.
- Ensure that you are familiar with your school's safeguarding policy and systems.

References and Bibliography

Bowlby, J. (1969) *Attachment. (Attachment and loss Volume 1).* Hogarth Press.

Department for Education (2025) *Keeping children safe in education: Statutory guidance for schools and colleges.* Available at https://www.gov.uk/government/publications/keeping-children-safe-in-education--2 (Accessed 26 January 2026).

Dweck, C. S. (2006) *Mindset: The new psychology of success.* Random House.

Panksepp, J. (2004) *Affective neuroscience: the foundations of human and animal emotions.* Oxford University Press.

Pierson, R. (2013) *Every kid needs a champion.* Available at https://www.ted.com/talks/rita_pierson_every_kid_needs_a_champion (Accessed 26 January 2026).

Rogers, C. R. and Freiberg, H. J. (1969) *Freedom to learn.* Charles Merrill.

Skinner, B. F. (1965) *Science and human behavior.* Simon and Schuster.

Van Nieuwerburgh, C. (2012) 'Coaching in education: An overview', in C. Van Nieuwerburgh (ed.), *Coaching in education: Getting better results for students, educators and parents.* pp. 3–24. Routledge.

3 Attendance and Punctuality

Joshua Speer

Introduction

It could be argued that attendance is the single most important factor within education, for two reasons. First, it is the most direct safeguarding measure which allows settings and professionals to support and keep a student safe; second, there's plenty of research which highlights how absence from education negatively impacts attainment. For example, the Department for Education (2025a) highlighted that a pupil who misses more days of school is likely to achieve worse grades in their GCSEs. In another report, the data goes down further, detailing that missing just ten days of Year 11 reduced the likelihood of grade 5 in English and Maths by around 50% (Department for Education, 2025b).

The chapter will try to take away from the contention of attendance concerns, such as school fines, and remind professionals that when it comes to supporting a student or family with attendance issues, there needs to be a balance between adopting both a behaviourist (reinforcement and punishment) and a humanist mindset (the student as a whole).

The Department for Education states: 'Successfully treating the root causes of absence and removing barriers to attendance, at home, in school or more broadly requires schools and local partners to work collaboratively in partnership with, not against families' (Department for Education, 2024a, p. 10). Additionally, my own local authority has issued guidance for all schools and colleges across the city (Brighton and Hove City Council, 2018). This policy offers a citywide approach

DOI: 10.4324/9781003620976-4

with how to engage and tackle behaviour through a relationship-first and trauma-informed lens. This balance also highlights how, for some students, being absent or displaying poor punctuality simply isn't their fault.

Attendance will likely fall within the remit of a tutor, largely due to the associated safeguarding and pastoral responsibilities. No student wakes up with disregard for education, school or college – at least, that's not what we'd like to think – but often there are some very complex situations connected with not attending. These could include:

- having poor mental health
- having poor physical health
- being a young carer
- having other responsibilities related to home (for example, needing to earn money or provide)
- coming from a background or household with low uptake or engagement with
- education
- bullying
- homelessness
- low income to pay for transport or have access to transport
- other examples outside of student control: A late bus, illness, family emergency, etc.

This list is not exhaustive and I'm sure you can think of many other reasons why a student might find attendance difficult. Often, as a tutor, you might have a deeper insight into the life of that student, which can really help in developing a positive relationship with them, enabling the tutor to be central in engaging (or re-engaging) a student with education. But how and what can be done? This chapter will unpack some of the important aspects related to attendance.

It's important to note that a lot of the writing and research in this chapter relates to post-Covid, as the rise in absenteeism has rocketed since the pandemic: 60% of UK teachers surveyed think absenteeism has worsened since the pandemic (Ismail, 2022). We can use this point as a re-evaluation of attendance practices.

Recordkeeping and Monitoring

As mentioned already, the tutor might be the first port of call when it comes to the attendance of a student. Whether identified by teachers, Head of Year, attendance team, safeguarding, or the tutor themselves, the tutor plays a crucial role in bridging the gap between school or college and where the young person resides.

It is a legal obligation for schools and colleges to correctly register a student and hold this record should it be required (Department for Education, 2024b). Attendance records might be called upon for safeguarding purposes or to highlight during an Ofsted inspection what a school or college is doing to tackle absences.

There are two ways of monitoring attendance:

- *Low attenders (Reactive):* These are students who are below the setting's required attendance threshold. The exact percentage will change based on your setting and government policy. Tackling this could be a termly letter home (or more frequent depending on auditing the data) or communication with parents/carers highlighting the school or college expectations.
- *Biggest drop (Proactive):* These are students who might be sitting within the above percentage ballpark but have had a significant percentage drop within a week or two. This relies on closer observations of data and being quick to 'nip in the bud' any issues which might be arising. The biggest or most rapid drops in attendance can be for myriad reasons, from personal circumstances to illness or unauthorised holiday. A significant and sudden drop requires further exploration by communicating with the student or parents/carers.

Both of these approaches are based on Nudge Theory (Thaler and Sunstein, 2021), a strategy used in behavioural economics to influence behavioural change in people. Nudge Theory is used within a cross-section of sectors from supermarkets to building design and government campaigns. It's also regularly used in education, just with little acknowledgement, with examples including the daily absence text or letter home each term: 'nudges include interventions that significantly alter the behaviour' (Thaler and Sunstein, 2021, p. 11). Research by

Chadeesingh and O'Mahoney (2025) highlighted that a text home at the start of each term detailing the amount of a young person's absence can increase attendance by 15 school days per 100 pupils across selected terms. If you're looking for how to use Nudge Theory in the classroom, I recommend the blog post by Ainsworth (2017).

'Nudging' should not be a large or taxing process and should not remove any choice or agency from an individual. Whilst Nudge Theory has had many positive impacts in education (Weijers, Koning and Paas, 2020), the long-term impacts in education aren't yet conclusive.

Whilst either of the above approaches are positive and either will align with a school or college policy to support attendance, I personally find a more proactive action is more beneficial. Additionally, whilst this won't be the role of a tutor, working closely with colleagues who also oversee attendance can develop a strong whole-setting culture.

A proactive approach is also echoed as a benefit to parent and carer engagement: 'Being proactive in liaising with parents is important, as it will enhance parental confidence and trust in the organisation' (O'Neill, 2021, p. 78). Engagement needs to consider the socioeconomic diversity of the school population and wider community, which might mean some parents/carers need further support to understand school or college processes.

Developing a positive parental engagement strategy is therefore key for buy-in. Imagine if the only time you communicated with home was when there were negative situations with a student, or you were utilising Nudge Theory for the gain of the setting with no acknowledgement of the positive rapport being developed between school or college and home. Contacting home on a regular basis to acknowledge and praise positive actions by a student will develop a strong rapport, which means that if contact home is made for negative reasons, there is already a relationship.

How to exactly produce regular communication can be quite simple, and most settings already do this through newsletters and parent communication emails, but other activities could include focus groups, parent surveys and effectively utilising parent governors to be the voice of parents at the school or college. If you're unsure how to develop a strategy for parental engagement, then I would consider looking up the CAPE model developed by Piotrowska et al. (2017). Emailing teachers to ask for a highlighted list of student names, where praise can be sent home, also strengthens the relationship between pastoral and teaching and learning.

If you're within a smaller school or college, or have further reaching responsibilities, then having email templates saved as a Word document which you can copy and paste for sending to parents/carers is an efficient way of managing your time and workload. Concerns? Praises? General check-in? All of these emails can be templates saved and ready to send. I would recommend spending a little time to ensure it's addressed using the student's name and not just 'student', as you want to create a sense of belonging and community with any communication. You also want to ensure it can be slightly edited for contextual information and available data.

Handling Repeated Poor Attendance

For a student to wake up and not want to go to school or college, or to not feel able to go, something has gone wrong. This 'something' could be a magnitude of things (see previous list), but it could also be to do with lacking motivation or not feeling represented, valued, or a sense of belonging.

Once a concern or issue has been highlighted, it's important to speak with that student as soon as possible to establish what is going on, or pass the information to relevant colleagues within the setting to investigate further.

It's important that any plan put in place for a student – or any actions to tackle poor attendance – is seen as supportive and never punitive. Even if the student goes through phases of poor and good attendance or seems to be the first name in your email inbox on a regular basis, a staff member telling them off or going straight through to detention is not going to increase their motivation or self-esteem. The ongoing checking-in and developing that rapport is key.

Motivation can be a driver and a common reason why some students start to drift away from education. See Chapter 9: Key Stage 4 Tutoring for more around this. Maybe they're studying a subject or unit which they just don't enjoy, or maybe their home situation is so large and complex that attendance to school or college really isn't on their radar. The issues facing students will differ depending on age and period of education they're engaged with; for example, a student taking the statutory GCSEs might find motivation more of a challenge as opposed to a college student who has actively chosen the subjects they're studying for two or three years.

It would be hard to mention motivation in the context of attendance without giving credit to Abraham Maslow. A household name for most educational professionals, his Hierarchy of Need (Maslow, 1943) gives rise to the principle that '[people] are given education that promotes growth' (Gravells, 2017, p. 90). The theory is a pyramid structure split into five areas: Physiological needs at the bottom (i.e. the most basic need), followed by safety and security, then recognition and belonging, followed by self-esteem and finally, self-actualisation. The focus is to support someone up the hierarchy by meeting their needs on each level, and who else best supports this than a tutor?

Getting the student re-engaged using methods or activities which relate to and motivate them is always a positive. What are that student's dreams or ambitions? Do they have a career in mind? What are their hobbies? Finding out this key information can really help with first, showing that you're interested and invested in that student, and second, provide avenues for exploring the importance of attendance, as well as showing an interest and developing a relationship with the student.

Working with a student to identify these interests and golden hooks can be a real win. This approach could be considered alongside Keller's (1983) ARCS model of motivation. ARCS stands for: Attention, Relevance, Confidence, and Satisfaction. Essentially, it's about finding the relevance for a learner so they can act with confidence and find satisfaction (Gravells, 2017). Additionally, a pastoral intervention such as a careers appointment or work experience can help a student to recognise the importance of soft skills and highlight the need for timekeeping and punctuality.

As we close this section, you might be wondering why there has been no mention of attendance rewards. What about the 100% certificates or other school-based incentives? Well, in short: The research isn't entirely convinced. **Rewards** when done well, can provide students with pride and a sense of accomplishment, plus they're also great for healthy competition. However, Shafer (2019) found that in a far-reaching study, there was no direct correlation between rewarding 100% attendance with prizes and yet a schools-based reward system does prove successful with positive impact for younger aged students (Robinson et al., 2021).

Punctuality

As already argued within other sections of this chapter, the rapport developed with students is stronger when an ethos of 'curious not furious' is adopted. Through the tracking and monitoring of student attendance, why is that student never on time for their first lesson? Your setting will have its own policies and approaches, but I feel that a score-card system of three issues with punctuality before some kind of intervention feels fair. Whilst schools and colleges should be a safe space for students to push boundaries, experiment and find their identity, we also need these spaces to mirror wider society and in doing so, prepare students for the workplace. Students need to be aware that arriving late to work continuously could lead to disciplinary action or even losing their job. As a tutor, why not work with your school/college careers advisor or careers leader, and when an employer comes in to speak about their workplace or sector, ask them to really press on the importance of punctuality.

Simply telling a student that they need to arrive on time or giving them a telling off when they're late solves little. Instead, through a conversation with the student, understanding why they're late is crucial.

To develop a whole-setting culture, students need to be active members; they are key stakeholders! As mentioned in the section above on motivation, activities which bring students into the conversation from a productive, engaging and relatable perspective can be positive. One such idea could be for students to create lateness prevention posters with tips for punctuality – this collaborative, peer-led learning not only provides the school or college with some positive student work but also embeds with the students the importance of arriving on time. Potter (2016) writes about this in more detail.

Additionally, as a tutor, sitting with students to look at:

- **Creating a timetable** for how to manage their out-of-school or college activities, allocating time for studies, whilst also balancing important social relationships such as hobbies and interests. It's important to strike the balance for wellbeing. For some students, just having something visual and tangible to highlight their organisation can be helpful.

- **Setting alarms**. This feels like a basic instruction for a student, but often it needs to be made obvious for them to realise. Most phones have clocks and in-built alarms, so getting students to set the alarms when in a meeting together displays a clear expectation of what you would like them to do moving forward.
- **Explaining the importance of a balanced diet**. Sweets and processed foods are fine in moderation, but eating a whole bar of chocolate before bed will spike the sugar and likely make it much harder for a student to fall asleep. Additionally, not eating a balanced diet could lead to being more susceptible to illness, which can also lead to attendance concerns. Impress the importance of good sleep hygiene such as switching off phones, going to bed at the same time, waking up at the same time and cutting any caffeine.
- **Engage with parents/carers**. Outside of the school or college, parents/carers are your biggest ally. If a student is up all night scrolling social media or gaming with friends, then your allies are those at home. Parental controls on devices or home internet can be used to enforce positive behaviours. Running parent/carer events or including information within newsletters relating to online safety or home controls can equip them with the confidence and skills to support their young person, as well as improve attendance and punctuality.

Emotional Based School Avoidance

Emotional Based School Avoidance (EBSA) is an umbrella term, encompassing a wide range of concerns or challenges a student might be facing related to attendance at school. Sometimes called Emotional Based School Non-Attendance (EBSNA), it has also been known as 'school phobia' or 'school refusal'. I have a personal issue with the final two terms as these tend to imply that a student is actively deciding not to attend or has the ability to make a choice, which is very rarely the case. This small section will focus on just two areas: W hat EBSA is and what role a tutor can play.

What Is EBSA?

EBSA is often situated within a complex web of personal circumstances or medical needs, which can impact both neurotypical and neurodivergent young people. Unlike common attendance concerns, EBSA is often rooted in prolonged periods of absence or distress related to attending education. It has been noted that Covid-19 really reset the situation and post-Covid absence at school has skyrocketed, with EBSA being much more common (Lester and Michelson, 2024).

Whilst EBSA can appear at any time, it is usually attributed to some kind of trauma or transition (Royal Free Hospital Children's School, n.d.). As a setting, it's therefore important that a student is given many opportunities to make themselves familiar with a new classroom, teacher(s) or even a whole new site if the transition is from school to college.

When considering the impact of EBSA, it's important to recognise the perpetuating issues this might cause a student: Anxious feelings about school/college lead to negative thoughts about school/college, which lead to avoidance of the situation causing anxiety. This in turn means that anxiety is reduced and therefore school/college is avoided more often, which amplifies anxious feelings about school or college (West Sussex Educational Psychology Service, 2022). Note that regardless of whether anxiety is a leading cause, anxiety and EBSA are often heavily linked.

The Tutor's Role

A tutor, often knowing students incredibly well through increased pastoral responsibilities, can play a leading role in supporting a student, their family and wider staff. For one, taking the time to get to know a student can mean that a trusted adult is present and on side. Additionally, putting in place transition activities for these students (open evenings, parent events, taster days, transition days, mini transition days, virtual meet and greet, etc.) will provide that student with much more familiarity. If working in a college, it's also worth considering getting out into feeder schools to run assemblies and/or workshops. A tutor might not be directly involved, but requesting to have input can have positive outcomes.

Very similar to tackling attendance more generally, EBSA can be most effectively challenged when there is a proactive approach: 'the longer the problems remain unaddressed, the poorer the outcome, as the difficulties and behaviours become entrenched' (West Sussex Educational Psychology Service, 2022, p. 13). One of the most important aspects related to this proactive approach is regularly speaking with colleagues, noticing small changes and getting the input of parents/carers. Regular meetings with all mentioned can ensure a safety net of support and signposting.

Do bear in mind that this support will look very different for each student. The reasons for EBSA will differ from each student and therefore having a standardised approach or fixed assessment method could be unfair for students or make them feel as if their needs are not being met.

Conclusion

Attendance is central to the successful learner journey. Whether using motivational theories to influence behavioural change, or practical tips to engage with students, this chapter has hopefully provided just a snapshot of what you could introduce or what you could develop or build upon within your setting. I have tried to focus on a relationships-first approach, ensuring that we acknowledge the power of holistic support.

Every setting and student person and their family are different – there is no one-size-fits-all approach when it comes to attendance.

- Sit with your attendance team to analyse data and highlight the biggest percentage drop. This can be a really beneficial way of seeing a tutor group or whole cohort of students and knowing whom to contact. Time is precious (and costly!) in education but adopting a proactive approach and ringfencing just 15 minutes every two weeks to sit with your attendance or reception team to find your top 5– 10 students can have long lasting benefits (and fewer attendance letters!)
- Consider how your parental engagement system currently operates. Do you have a policy or approach? Are parents/carers only hearing from you when things aren't going so well?

- Take a look at the Education Endowment Fund's Supporting School Attendance Reflection and Planning Tool (Education Endowment Fund, 2024). This is a great exercise to audit areas of strength and areas for further development.

References and Bibliography

Ainsworth, P. (2017) *Changing classrooms: One nudge at a time.* Available at https://www.teachertoolkit.co.uk/2017/03/11/changing-classrooms-one-nudge-at-a-time/ (Accessed 23 July 2025).

Brighton and Hove Inclusion Support Services (2018) *Developing an attachment aware behaviour regulation policy: Guidance for Brighton & Hove schools September 2018.* Available at https://ww3.brighton-hove.gov.uk/sites/brighton-hove.gov.uk/files/Behaviour%20Regulation%20Policy%20Guidance%20-%20Sep%2018_1.pdf (Accessed 28 May 2025).

Centre for Young Lives (2025) *Beyond the classroom: The role of enrichment in tackling the school absence crisis.* Available at https://www.centreforyounglives.org.uk/news-centre/new-research-reveals-positive-link-between-enrichment-and-tackling-the-school-attendance-crisis (Accessed 7 April 2025).

Chadeesingh, L. and O'Mahoney, C. (2025) *It all adds up: How better communication can lead to better school attendance.* Available at https://www.bi.team/blogs/it-all-adds-up-how-small-changes-in-communication-can-lead-to-better-school-attendance/ (Accessed 19 December 2025).

Department for Education (2024a) *Working together to improve school attendance: Statutory guidance for maintained schools, academies, independent schools and local authorities.* Available at https://assets.publishing.service.gov.uk/media/66bf300da44f1c4c23e5bd1b/Working_together_to_improve_school_attendance_-_August_2024.pdf (Accessed 7 April 2025).

Department for Education (2024b) *Summary table of responsibilities for school attendance: Statutory guidance for maintained schools, academies, independent schools, and local authorities.* Available at https://assets.publishing.service.gov.uk/media/66bf301e253aee7aafdbdfea/Summary_table_of_responsibilities_for_school_attendance_-_August_2024.pdf (Accessed 12 January 2026).

Department for Education (2025a) *The impact of school absence on lifetime earnings.* Available at https://assets.publishing.service.gov.uk/media/67d2cf8f4702aacd2251cbae/The_impact_of_school_absence_on_lifetime_earnings.pdf (Accessed 7 April 2025).

Department for Education (2025b) *The link between attendance and attainment in an assessment year.* Available at https://assets.publishing.service.gov.uk/media/67c96d7dd0fba2f1334cf2ed/The_link_between_attendance_and_attainment_in_an_assessment_year_-_March_2025.pdf (Accessed 7 April 2025).

Education Endowment Foundation (2024) *Supporting school attendance.* Available at https://educationendowmentfoundation.org.uk/education-evidence/leadership-and-planning/supporting-attendance (Accessed 15 December 2025).

Gravells, A. (2017) *Principles and practices of teaching and training: A guide for teachers and trainers in the FE and skills sector.* Sage.

Hill, J. (2025) *Attending to the problem.* Available at https://feweek.co.uk/attending-to-the-problem/ (Accessed 9 April 2025).

Ismail, A. (2022) *Absenteeism: How we'll rebuild a culture of school attendance.* Available at https://schoolsweek.co.uk/absenteeism-how-well-rebuild-a-culture-of-school-attendance/ (Accessed 19 December 2025).

Keller, J. M. (1983). 'Motivational design of instruction', in C. M. Reigeluth (ed.), *Instructional design theories and models: An overview of their current status.* Erlbaum, pp. 383–436.

Lester, K.J. and Michelson, D. (2024) 'Perfect storm: Emotionally based school avoidance in the post-COVID-19 pandemic context', *British Medical Journal Mental Health*, 27(1). Available at doi: 10.1136/bmjment-2023-300944 (Accessed 12 January 2026).

Maslow, A. (1943) 'A theory of human motivation', *Psychological Review*, 50(4), pp.370–396. Available at https://psycnet.apa.org/doiLanding?doi=10.1037%2Fh0054346 (Accessed 12 January 2026).

O'Neill, M. (2021) *Proactive pastoral care: Nurturing happy, healthy and successful learners.* Bloomsbury.

Piotrowska, P., Tully, L., Lenroot, R. and Kimonis, E. (2017) 'Mothers, fathers and parental systems: A conceptual model of parental engagement in programmes for child mental health – connect, attend, participate, enact (CAPE)', *Clinical Child and Family Psychology Review*, 20(2), pp. 146–161. Available at https://link.springer.com/content/pdf/10.1007/s10567-016-0219-9.pdf (Accessed 12 January 2026).

Potter, M. (2016) *100 Ideas for secondary teachers: Tutor time.* Bloomsbury.

Robinson, C.D., Gallus, J., Lee, M.G. and Rogers, D. (2021) *The demotivating effect (and unintended message) of awards.* Available at https://www.sciencedirect.com/science/article/abs/pii/S0749597818306083?via%3Dihub (Accessed 12 January 2026).

Royal Free Hospital Children's School (n.d.) *Emotionally based school avoidance.* Available at https://www.royalfree.camden.sch.uk/page/?title=EBSA&pid=120 (Accessed 7 April 2025).

Shafer, L. (2019) *How attendance awards backfire: New research shows that awards intended to motivate can do the opposite.* Available at https://www.gse.harvard.edu/ideas/usable-knowledge/19/07/how-attendance-awards-backfire (Accessed 7 April 2025).

Sims, C. (2024) *The drivers behind attendance: What we are learning about the importance of belonging, engagement, sanctions and support.* Available at https://my.chartered.college/impact_article/the-drivers-behind-attendance-what-we-are-learning-about-the-importance-of-belonging-engagement-sanctions-and-support/ (Accessed 10 September 2025).

Thaler, R. H. and Sunstein, C. R. (2022) *Nudge: The final edition*. Penguin.

Weijers, R. J., Koning, B. and Paas, F. (2020) 'Nudging in education: From theory towards guidelines for successful implementation', *European Journal of Psychology of Education*, 36, pp. 893–902. Available at doi: 10.1007/s10212-020-00495-0 (Accessed 12 January 2026).

West Sussex Educational Psychology Service (2022) *Emotionally based school avoidance: Good practice guidance for schools and support agencies*. Available at https://schools.westsussex.gov.uk/Services/3282 (Accessed 15 December 2025).

4 Making the Most of Form Time

Sanum J. Khan

Introduction

I found being a form tutor the hardest thing to let go of once I moved into senior leadership. I learnt so much about time management, building relationships, parent/carer engagement and whole-school vision in this role and truly enjoyed it. In some cases, the senior leadership team (SLT) wrote a full programme that all teachers must follow. In others, tutors have been given full autonomy to plan the time as they see fit. Being a form tutor is a huge privilege; welcoming a group of young people every day, celebrating their wins and ensuring they know they belong, are seen and are valued. In this chapter, I share some of the key things I have learnt to make this time as effective as possible.

The Importance of Planning

Tutor time must be carefully planned to ensure that students benefit. If tutor time is first thing in the morning and not carefully planned, it may contribute to persistent lateness to school. Wherever it is in the day, it is a part of the predictable routines that give students security and a sense of safety. It is a period of the day where students are asked to engage and therefore must be approached with the same high level of care as curriculum content is.

You may have **routines** for the week that are dictated by the Senior Team/Head of Year. Sticking to these **routines** is an important way of offering consistency. It supports any students who may end up moving

DOI: 10.4324/9781003620976-5

tutor groups or are new to the school with settling in and, of course, makes processes for cover in your absence smooth. Colquhoun (2023, p. 50) writes that 'if wellbeing is at the forefront of our focus in the classroom, then creating predictable **routines** is the vehicle to assist the journey', with particular emphasis on the value of **routines** for students experiencing anxiety and stress. Colquhoun (2023) also notes that **routines** free students from the uncertainty around procedures and encourage brain power towards learning.

Routines of the week – such as which day assembly is on and that you must do a uniform check daily – may be dictated by school leaders. However, you can also adopt tutor time **routines** of your own, nurturing a culture with your tutor group that is aligned with the school values and expectations. For example, instead of reading the student notices to the students you could create a rota where they all have a turn in reading them out for everyone to hear. Instead of doing a uniform check and register as two separate events, you could ask the students to stand behind their chairs for the register and check their uniform as you call the register out. If lining up for assembly is important, spend time in the first week ensuring students all know the register order and rehearsing their line-up as they wait to come into the tutor room. This planning for culture and **routines** is imperative; consciously nurturing it leads to success. Mccrea (2020) proposes that **routines** that create space for learning are one of the core drivers of motivation in learning. Given the regularity of tutor time sessions, running **routines** here can therefore be a significant contributor to the motivation levels in students at school.

Any adaptations to school routines you make should be shared with the Head of Year or SLT. Autonomy is valuable, but so is consistency. Sometimes there are non-negotiable elements of tutor time that are part of a bigger picture, such as attendance, safeguarding, establishing school routines and literacy. It's important that any adjustments you make do not conflict with year group or school priorities.

PSHE in Tutor Time

You may find that you are asked to teach PSHE during tutor time. If the curriculum content and pedagogy are new to you, this can feel daunting. PSHE is a valuable 'curriculum for life' that is best delivered by trusted staff at the school (Barksfield, 2018). Therefore, planning the sessions is even more important and can mean undertaking training or observing others as part of the planning process. There are resources widely available online, but be sure to access ones that are consistent with the school's culture and practices. You might find that the school pays for membership to some organisations to inform PSHE planning and it is worthwhile spending some time with the PSHE Lead and your line manager to identify how this membership can benefit you. Knowing the topics in advance and knowing your tutees is key; a child experiencing racism will not experience your lessons on identity and belonging in the same way someone not experiencing racism will. Equally, the perpetrator of racism may well be in the room and so careful planning (adjusting the seating plan, speaking to individual students and parents/carers ahead of the lesson, depersonalising content and having rigorous and thoughtful resources) is key. **Relationships** are at the core of good preparation for delivering PSHE in tutor time. See Chapter 5: Teaching Personal, Social, Health & Economic Education (PSHE) for a more detailed exploration of this.

Social time

Chapter 1: Knowing Your Form – The Foundation of Relational Education explores suggestions of how to get to know who is in your form. This is an ongoing process and the **relationships** element of the **6Rs** cannot be ticked off once you have learnt names, read Special Education Needs and Disabilities (SEND), Educational Health and Care Plans (EHCPs) or other medical care plans, read attainment data and looked at current behaviour and achievement data. Social time is another important way to get to know your students and should be planned to improve relationships within the group as much as with you.

Building 'ice breaker' tasks into tutor time, regularly reviewing the seating plan and welcoming students in at the door are important ways to build a sense of community. Colquhoun (2025) offers over 100 activities tutors can try with their forms which contribute towards relationships, routines, academic success and student wellbeing. Introducing new ideas needs to be balanced against the impact of disrupting **routines**, so introduce new things at a time of the year where you feel they have the most chance of success. For example, the final week of term, on a drop-down day or event day or in a week where many students are out on a trip will not set the new ideas up for success.

It can also be helpful to use student voice to plan social and wellbeing activities. For example, I once introduced 'news-day Tuesday' with a group who regularly talked about fake news. The idea was that three people could pick news stories of the week – all of which had to be true – and the class voted on the one they liked the most. This was sometimes because it was so absurd they couldn't believe it was true, it was heartwarming or uplifting, or it celebrated something important to them (such as a sporting win). At that school, students were not allowed in classrooms unless supervised by a staff member but my form group wanted to be able to use indoor space. Once a week, I agreed to have my lunch in my room (which forced me to tidy my desk!) whilst the students played table tennis by pushing tables together and using a pop-up net. They arranged a rota of play and worked together to ensure the room was clean and tidy before the end of lunch. This also meant that tutees knew where to find me if they needed a chat.

In addition to this, Hammond (2015) outlines the value of talk structures in maximising engagement. Not only do varied talk structures improve relationships, but they build intellectual capacity and thus improve academic outcomes. As a tutor, you have the power to closely knit the academic and pastoral parts of school life for your students, and embracing varied talk structures is one way to achieve that (bringing together both the **rigour** and the **receptive** elements of the **6Rs**). Hammond (2015, p. 149) highlights that some cultural talk structures favour 'social talk structures' where the participants actively engage 'through vocalization, motion or movement as they are speaking'. It is also called rapport-talk, and embracing this contributes positively to relationships in tutor time. Equally, you will soon identify which students favour 'academic talk structures' that rely on instructional conversation and this can help you understand why some students achieve well in some lessons but not in others. Greeting them at the door, learning names quickly and having a 'warm up chat' as you get the register opened up are all ways of introducing social talk structures in tutor time.

Working With Student Leaders

Student leadership is a key part of personal development and leadership across year groups contributes well to this. You may be allocated student ambassadors for short-term work with your tutor group, such as student council representatives, prefects, buddies, wellbeing ambassadors or academic mentors. If you are allocated student ambassadors, they are important role models for your tutees but they do need to be guided in order to ensure their time with your tutor group is effective.

If you have been assigned buddies or student leaders, the staff member overseeing them may have written a programme for them to follow. This might include activities and tasks and you should check these yourself ahead of time. Enlarging the font, adding subtitles or translating key words is as important here as it is in any curriculum lesson for students who require adaptations. The programme writer will not know the individual needs of the students in your form group but you will – be sure to use this knowledge as power to set student leaders up for success.

Equally, make time to introduce the student leaders to the class and be fully present throughout. Close the laptop lid, join in with the activities and support with behaviour management whilst encouraging positive engagement from the class. If you can see the student leaders are struggling to complete their set programme skillfully, offer supportive feedback and suggest that you team-teach the next one until their confidence grows. Publicly praise the student leaders for their successes too so that the class sees the student leaders' achievements being celebrated. This will contribute to a sense of community in your tutor group and, as per the **6Rs**, it shows your tutees that you are **reliable**; you want them to have an excellent experience regardless of who is leading the session.

If a programme of delivery has not been given to the buddies, here is a list of things that you could direct them to:

- Leading a weekly task (such as a short quiz of the news of the week).
- Working with a small group of students to write and deliver a tutor time presentation (perhaps on a national theme of that week).
- Offering peer-mentoring to some students in a small group.

- Answering questions or responding to comments that students submit in advance about school life (which you will need to read and filter before sharing with the student leaders to ensure they are appropriate and that any questions that cause concern are addressed directly by you and/or shared with the Designated Safeguarding Lead).
- Running a competition.

Reading

There is lots of literature and research on the benefits of reading and changing reading habits of young people. In this section, I will be assuming we all agree that reading is beneficial for both academic success and wellbeing. I'll also be assuming that reading in tutor time is more of a help than a hindrance.

You may have a reading book and time allocation dictated to you by the school. Even if this isn't how you would choose to do it, it's important that you roll the programme out as instructed. Often, such initiatives rely on evidence-informed strategies and are part of a wider literacy and/or wellbeing focus. If things aren't working, be sure to give specific and kindly worded feedback with potential solutions to make it better. This advice extends to all areas of a tutor programme, but in my experience reading is often the one area that encourages the widest range of views amongst tutors.

If students are given autonomy on what they read but told that they must read during at least one tutor time per week, for example, take note of who is reading what. If anyone is reading something you have read, use this as an opportunity to strike up a conversation about what you liked and didn't like about it. Invite students to give reviews to the class of books they have loved and would recommend to others. Importantly, role-model reading and take some of this tutor time to sit and read as well.

Reluctant readers can offer a whole range of avoidance tactics with reading. These can include having the same book for weeks (but never completing it), changing the book weekly because they didn't like the previous one, often forgetting their book or wanting to read online. Whilst these may be genuine explanations, you should explore the potential that the student just is not reading outside of lessons. You may need to refer to your Literacy Lead, the student's English or Reading teacher or the school librarian for some support here. I used to also keep a printout of a selection of short stories that could be read in 15 minutes; any student who forgot their book could complete one of these instead.

According to the National Literacy Trust (2025), young readers fall into one of three categories: Curious readers (who see reading as valuable when they learn something from the text), mindful readers (who read because it improves their wellbeing) and social readers (who read to connect with issues they care about, the wider world or other people). When encouraging students to try new things to read, it is helpful to ask questions about what they enjoy watching or doing as this may help narrow down the options. Reluctant readers, for example, are more inclined to choose reading that links to TV they are watching or books that match their personal interests.

One final comment about reading is that the range of things students can read is huge. Non-fiction improves literacy and should be included in your 'reading for pleasure' lists. For the 'curious reader' this is a valuable category. Equally, short stories, poems, articles and blogs are all valuable for students to read. In a previous school, I worked with the librarian to order books that were short (my students could read them in 35 minutes) but with a high reading age to maintain the academic challenge. We found that the commitment of a novel and the ability to retain content and make inferences was overwhelming for some. Short stories reduced this, encouraged completion and a sense of achievement, and prompted a desire in the students to continue reading.

Emotional Intelligence

For much of this chapter I have explored what you can do to make the most of tutor time for students. In this section, I'll be bringing in another focus: How to make the most out of tutor time for yourself.

Emotional intelligence is an important part of **relationships**, effective learning and positive culture in schools. Roberts (2022, p. 34) asserts that 'treating others with respect, dignity and compassion should be the core foundations of all teaching and leadership styles'.

Your role as a tutor should be seen as that of a leader. Your tutor group is the team, you are the leader and emotional intelligence is integral to your success.

In addition, Jones and Macpherson (2021) outline the case for progress in teaching to be viewed not only as a promotion to a more senior role but also as being more effective and skilled in your current role. Nurturing a sense of emotional intelligence serves both of these aims because it is a skill that is needed in abundance the more senior you become in a school. Here are some ways in which this can be nurtured as a form tutor:

- You want to be a leader for the tutor group but the goal is their growth, achievement and fulfilment. When you celebrate the wins and, in my case, get competitive about House competitions, remember that you are doing it so that they buy into it.
- **Be adaptive**. Whilst social talk may help bring some students in, it can be uncomfortable territory for others. Circulate the room, greet at the door, have one-to-one conversations as well as addressing the whole class. It's easy to notice the students who speak often and most loudly but it's imperative that you notice those who might otherwise go unnoticed and adapt your practice to bring them in too.
- **Be receptive**. In particular, respond appropriately to wider issues that the tutor group may be facing. This can include staff members leaving, local disasters, upcoming mock exams or global affairs. Student leaders can be helpful in supporting some of these (for example, running sessions on effective revision strategies). Others may require deeper learning for you and collaboration with other members of the school. In one of my roles as a tutor, I saw the impact that conflict in the Middle East was having on my students so I worked with the history and politics department to put on a lunchtime forum to create a discussion space for students.
- When you receive emails about your tutees missing deadlines, displaying poor behaviour for learning or otherwise not meeting expectations, don't get defensive. Use collective language with the tutor group to show them that you are in it together. For example, 'What can we do differently?' or 'How are we going to repair the relationship with that teacher?'

- **Be clear**. As Brown (2018) tells us, clear is kind and unclear is unkind. Ensure your instructions are clear – which may mean offering them verbally as well as written down. This might be in the form of a class contract or, as in my school, reminders with deadlines on Google Classroom. This clarity extends to your consistency: Being **reliable** is one of the **6Rs** that is most important here. If you tell tutees they will receive a sanction for repeated missing uniform, ensure you actually issue the sanction. The same applies to **rewards**. Lack of consistency can be viewed as lack of clarity and this is unkind.

Of course, anything you role model here will act as a good example to students and the way you show and grow your emotional intelligence will, in turn, create aspirational character goals for your tutees. Nurturing emotional intelligence results in wins all round!

- Identify the current tutor time routines and expectations in your school.
- Identify the Head of Year and other leaders who are linked to your year group. Speak to them about what their vision for tutor time is and take this on board for anything you plan to do – consistency and coherence need to be carefully balanced.
- If you are teaching PSHE, identify CPD you can undertake to do this well. This may include watching other tutors teach it first.
- Social time is still planned time: Think carefully about talk structures and how you use these to build relationships.
- Remember that, as a form tutor, you are a leader. Nurture your leadership.

References and Bibliography

Barksfield, J. (2018) *The seven myths of PSHE education*. Available at https://www.sec-ed.co.uk/content/best-practice/the-seven-myths-of-pshe-education/ (Accessed 24 July 2025).

Brown, B. (2018) *Dare to lead: Brave work, tough conversations, whole hearts*. Random House.

Colquhoun, K. (2023) *A practical guide to pupil wellbeing: Strategies for classroom teachers.* John Catt.

Colquhoun, K. (2025) *Transforming your tutor time curriculum: 100+ activities to support wellbeing, strengthen culture and supercharge success.* Routledge.

Hammond, Z. (2015) *Culturally responsive teaching and the Brain: Promoting authentic engagement and rigor among culturally and linguistically diverse students.* Corwin.

Jones, K. and Macpherson, R. (2021) *The teaching life.* John Catt.

Mccrea, P. (2020) *Motivated teaching.* Self-published.

National Literacy Trust (2025) *Reading report 2025: Rethinking reading for pleasure in schools.* Available at https://literacytrust.org.uk/training-and-workshops/teachbrief/rethinking-reading-for-pleasure-in-schools/ (Accessed 24 July 2025).

Roberts, N. C. (2022) *The emotionally intelligent teacher.* Bloomsbury.

5 Teaching Personal, Social, Health and Economic Education (PSHEE)

Sophie-Lauren McPhee

Introduction

PSHEE is a bit like your favourite pet – it has many variations on its name: PHSE, PSHCE, Life Lessons, Learning For Life, and numerous others. In addition to that, there's FBVs (Fundamental British Values), SMSC (Spiritual, Moral, Social and Cultural) development and PD (Personal Development). For the sake of simplicity, this chapter will use 'PSHEE' as a shorthand for tutor time sessions that cover the three core themes of the PSHE Association's Programme of Study (PSHE Association, n.d., p. 2): Health and Wellbeing, Relationships and Living in the Wider World. The same principles can be applied, however, if your school teaches subjects often bundled with PSHEE through the tutor time format, such as Citizenship and Religious Education.

I imagine that PSHEE is unlikely to be your subject specialism, and not something you are able to devote much time to in terms of planning and pedagogy, which is why this chapter aims to equip you with some basic principles you can use not only to underpin your PSHEE teaching, but also to guide you in your relationships with pupils in general. As a trainee psychotherapist, I use child development and therapeutic principles as my frame of reference. This is not quite the same as trauma-informed practice, although that is certainly a part of it. Of course, I am not advocating for every form tutor to become

DOI: 10.4324/9781003620976-6

a part-time therapist to their tutees, but this chapter is likely to appeal more greatly to those teachers wanting to work with a relational, rather than a behaviourist, approach. Adolescents are more likely to embrace social and emotional guidance from an adult they trust, whom they look up to and whom they feel has a genuine interest in their holistic development as human beings; therefore a different approach is needed from when you are teaching your subject specialism.

The Case for Form Tutors Teaching PSHEE

If I could summarise this whole book in one tip, it would be this: Love your tutees. Greet them, show an interest in them, observe them, monitor them, say goodbye to them, be obviously *in loco parentis.* I am writing this the day after our school's open evening event. A boy from my Year 8 form popped in to say hello between music performances and I was telling a group of parents how teaching PSHEE really channels my 'mother energy'. When I said that I 'mother' my pupils, the boy nodded vigorously and said, 'She really does!' That is exactly what I'm aiming for, both as a form tutor and a PSHEE teacher. It's okay to love them, and it's right to parent them.

Why do I say this? Of course, we are not looking to replace the parent figures they already have. However, whether you are yet fully invested in the idea or not, you *are* a parent figure to them, and for some members of your tutor group, you may be the only **reliable** adult they have in their lives. Yet, even if they do have a loving and stable home with excellent parenting, you are still someone who will form part of what in Transactional Analysis psychotherapy we call the 'Parent ego state' (Berne, 1961); i.e. a pattern of thoughts, feelings and behaviours that we internalise from our parents, caregivers and other parent-figures, such as teachers. Therefore, we must be exceedingly careful about what we pass on to them.

As possibly the closest thing they have to a parent-figure in school, you are the best person to be teaching your tutees PSHEE, a subject which for me is synonymous with parenting. However, you are only going to be the best person as far as you are committed to developing **relationships** with your tutees: 'For a child to be open to being parented by an adult, he must be actively attaching to that adult, be wanting contact and closeness with him' (Neufeld and Maté, 2024, p. 6). Once they have developed a secure attachment to you, they will be more **receptive** to what you are teaching them. Furthermore, they will more likely feel safe to express thoughts and opinions in PSHEE lessons, and make a safeguarding disclosure to you if necessary. It has been shown that the quality of the relationship between therapist and client is a strong indicator of the success of therapy (Flückiger et al., 2018); I would argue that the same applies for PSHEE: Whilst not therapy of course, they share the same goal of fostering the personal development of the individual.

This last point could be used to argue the case for teacher–pupil relationship as being more important than the PSHEE subject knowledge of the individual member of staff. As a PSHEE subject specialist, I do not want to be misinterpreted as saying that you can get away with insecure knowledge: PSHEE, like every other subject taught in school, must have **rigour**, and with this subject giving out incorrect information could even be life-threatening. (If you think this is an exaggeration, consider that in PSHEE we teach about First Aid and harmful substances, for example). Having worked as a subject specialist who at one point was teaching every pupil in the school, however, it is virtually impossible to know every pupil well. Yet with your form group you can have regular contact with your Head of Year, who should inform you of any matters of pastoral concern within your group and you can follow up on any issues arising in your PSHEE lessons with particular pupils much more easily.

In short, a key purpose of your role as form tutor is to monitor and drive forward the personal, social and emotional development of your pupils. Whilst it is important for PSHEE to have the same status as examined subjects in terms of **rigour** and **routines**, when delivered by you it contributes to the overview you have of their holistic development. PSHEE comprises an extremely broad vista of topics, so you cannot possibly know everything you need to teach straight away; however a commitment to ongoing professional learning, starting with the basic principles below, will serve your pupils well.

Techniques for Teaching PSHEE Well

It is really important to understand that cultivating excellent **relationships** with your tutees does not mean being their friend – it is possible to show an interest in what they got up to at the weekend, for example, whilst still maintaining a professional distance. If you consider that teaching PSHEE involves sex and relationship education, professional boundaries are imperative – to safeguard you as well as them. Personal stories can enhance the lesson by allowing pupils to learn from your experience, but you *must* exercise professional judgement on this, remembering that any information you choose to share in the classroom could be published on social media or misinterpreted. Sharing your experience preparing for and attending a job interview is likely to be safer than discussing your experience of poor mental health, for example. Hopefully it goes without saying that any in-depth sharing of your personal relationships should be strictly off-limits. Whilst sharing life experience can be part of the job, we must always remember that we are working with human beings whose brains are not fully developed yet and are still learning about managing impulse and decision-making.

For this reason, creating a contract with your pupils for PSHEE lessons provides an important foundation for your work together. Elsewhere, you may see this concept referred to as 'ground rules', but I prefer 'contract' as it implies equality of all parties involved, both in its creation and its execution. For example, if we all agree to keep what is said in the lesson within the classroom, then you too must adhere to it, and not laugh at a pupil's mistake over coffee at break. Moreover, calling it a contract lends gravitas and therefore makes it more likely to be adhered to, unlike 'learning agreement', a term which perhaps older pupils may feel too grown up for. Having a contract in your PSHEE classroom is one way in which the learning environment can be made more **reliable**. This is really important for all pupils, given the sensitive topics that will be covered, but especially important for pupils with SEND.

So what needs to be covered in your contract? The pupils themselves are likely to contribute all of the obvious elements, such as active listening and not ridiculing others. However, it is also important to consider the following:

- What you will do if you do not know the answer to a pupil's question, or feel uncomfortable answering it.
- That no assumptions will be made about someone based on what they say in PSHEE lessons – including assumptions about you, the teacher.

- How it will be reinforced that PSHEE is of equal importance to their other subjects, so the same expectations with regard to behaviour **routines** and **rigour** apply – and that includes you! If you turn up to the lesson confident about the high-quality materials you are delivering, the pupils are more likely to buy into what you are teaching them.
- What will you do if someone breaks the contract? Often, this will be a case of following your school's normal sanction procedures, but professional curiosity about the communication behind the behaviour is also advised.

Having a learning contract is one way of cultivating *psychological safety* in the classroom. Another useful tool is using your school's online learning platform, such as Google Classroom or MS Teams, to share the learning objectives for the lesson in advance. This gives pupils the opportunity to do some research or reading before the lesson so that they can contribute with confidence, but importantly, gives them the opportunity to speak to you if they think they might feel vulnerable in the lesson. Hopefully, it is part of the wider school culture that parents and carers also monitor this online platform. Whilst some pupils may be reserved about coming forward, their caregivers may be more proactive. Caregiver engagement and partnership is crucial in PSHEE – whilst you are not responsible for this (the Head of Department is), forging a good home–school partnership can be something everyone contributes to and forms part of general safeguarding. If, however, a parent or carer requests to see lesson materials, please refer on to the PSHEE Lead so that there is a consistent approach to this situation. The government's 'Relationships Education, Relationships and Sex Education and Health Education Guidance' states that schools should 'be transparent with parents about all materials used in RSHE' (Department for Education, 2025, p. 5). Given that there have been very strong feelings from the general public about the Relationships and Sex Education curriculum in recent years, it is vital that any requests and queries from parents and carers are referred on to someone who is adequately trained to handle such delicate matters and has a thorough knowledge of what makes excellent PSHEE.

Creating psychological safety, as mentioned, forms part of safeguarding the children in your care. How you act in relationship with your pupils will give them a psychological message about whether you are a safe adult to whom they can make a disclosure should they need it. This is important no matter which subject you are teaching, but in PSHEE there is a higher chance of you needing to contact your school's Designated Safeguarding Lead (DSL). Be acutely aware of pupils' non-verbal responses to sensitive topics, such as their body language or facial expressions, and pass on any concerns, no matter how small. Refer any inappropriate or concerning comments made in your lesson to your DSL so that they can investigate, even if it appears that the pupil is joking. A DSL is likely to prefer to get 100 referrals and 99 of them turn out to be a false alarm than miss the one child in need of help. The use of appropriate, respectful language needs to be covered in your learning contract and at this point you can explicitly state to pupils that inappropriate behaviour may be treated as a safeguarding concern if you deem it necessary.

This section can only provide you with a mere snapshot of what it means to teach PSHEE well, and ideally will not be the only training you receive. If it is not possible for you to attend CPD or inset on this, then I recommend *Developing Quality PSHE In Secondary Schools and Colleges* (McPhee and Pugh, 2024), which provides a much more in-depth exploration of how to make PSHEE safe and, chapter by chapter, gives guidance on how to teach each topic within PSHEE well. It also contains guidance on creating a PSHEE curriculum, so would be especially suitable if you are aspiring to subject leadership or a senior pastoral role that incorporates responsibility for PSHEE one day.

Potential Challenges

Despite the wealth of support out there, including that mentioned above, the biggest challenge in PSHEE, even as a subject specialist, is keeping up with subject knowledge. Whilst the PSHEE Lead is officially responsible for providing up-to-date materials, proactive reading and research on your part will mean that you are more confident in the classroom, which in turn will increase psychological safety for your learners. It's common sense, if you think about it – why would children take advice from someone who doesn't sound sure of what they're talking about?

However, to be an effective PSHEE teacher you do not need to know every single detail for every single topic. For example, when teaching about drugs, knowing the specifics about all different types of drugs is less important than doing your research into the most consumed drugs and focussing on them, or looking at general principles of resisting peer pressure, safety plans and harm reduction measures.

Remember also that you have life experience. This doesn't mean that you need to tell pupils your life story, but you can reflect privately on what you have learned from your experiences and find a way to pass them on to pupils without necessarily revealing that your life is the source of the advice. Do not forget, too, that the pupils will have thoughts and ideas that they can teach you, based on their frame of reference. Whilst it would not be appropriate for them to share their own experiences with you (unless privately making a safeguarding disclosure), you can learn from them in terms of hearing about what is important to a young person in this part of the 21st century (or indeed, a person who is different to you in other ways, such as gender, religion, ethnicity, etc.), which in turn can inform your teaching of that same topic in the future. Inviting pupils to speak up also reinforces the message that their voice is important, that there is space for it and that it is safe to do so.

Hopefully, you are already reading or watching the news regularly and always have a book on the go. I have found simply reading widely adds immensely to the repository of information I pass on to pupils in PSHEE lessons, even if it is sometimes 'off the cuff' and not planned into the lesson specifically. Keeping up with the news means keeping up with the latest developments within society that might be affecting our pupils – this is wise to do generally as a teacher, so that you maintain an awareness of factors that might be impacting pupils' attainment, behaviour and attendance. Of course, we must also use our own critical thinking when it comes to using news stories and not be reactive when it comes to warning young people about the latest danger that the headlines are screaming about.

Finally, with regard to subject knowledge, do not underestimate what the pupils can teach you. You can come to the lesson armed with the latest research on a given topic, but you don't know what it's like to be a young person of this generation – and that's where their expertise comes in. Enjoy learning about the latest slang and the hottest trends – this gives you an insight into their frame of reference and what's important to them. That in turn allows you to update your PSHEE materials to make them more current.

Framing pupils as experts is one way of increasing pupil buy-in when it comes to PSHEE. It is possible that because PSHEE is a non-examined subject (i.e. does not eventually lead to a qualification) and in a lot of schools is not taught by specialists, your tutees will get the idea that it is somehow less important. Not so: Public Health England produced a report in 2014 collating evidence that greater pupil health and wellbeing is linked to greater achievement (Public Health England, 2014). Therefore, your pupils need to understand that PSHEE provides the foundation upon which academic success is built.

Using **rewards** can help here. Obviously, your school will have a House Point or commendation system, but I have used other types of rewards to motivate my learners. For example, you may be surprised about the appeal of stickers for pupils of this age – especially scented or glittery ones – even at Key Stage 5! The stickers can be awarded for anything you choose, but I tend to give them out if someone demonstrates evidence of critical thinking, offers an insight that I had not considered or demonstrates engagement with the material beyond what might ordinarily be expected for the age group. The use of scenarios is a great way to encourage critical thinking and discussion, but it is best to consult a PSHEE specialist as to the scenario's suitability. Scenarios also offer a way of making the learning relevant, by offering real-world application beyond exam and job success. The great thing about PSHEE is that so much of what we cover has a wide-ranging impact on pupils' personal and professional lives. Stating that explicitly can help pupils understand why it is (in my opinion) the most important subject in school. For example, recently I was emphasising to my pupils why 'paying attention' was a crucial life skill: Not simply so one does not break school rules or can do well in exams, but because by learning to pay attention to others they will learn how to treat someone the way they wish to be treated, and by learning how to direct their attention inwards it will help them know if they feel unsafe.

- Get a copy of the curriculum overview for tutor time at your school, identify areas of subject development for you and familiarise yourself with the materials used.
- Meet with the relevant pastoral lead at your school to identify any pupils in your form group who may feel vulnerable

during specific tutor time sessions and make a plan for how you can ensure psychological safety as far as possible.
- Make sure your school has a copy of the 'PSHE Toolkit' series by Speechmark. This is a collection of books being published from 2026 onwards comprising full lesson plans for Key Stages 3, 4 and 5 plus tutor time materials for all topics within PSHEE, written by experienced professionals in the field.
- Book onto the PSHE Association's training events for teaching PSHEE effectively. This would be an excellent opportunity for you to then cascade the training to the rest of the form tutor team.
- Build a network of educators with expertise in the field via LinkedIn. This gives you ready-made sources of support if and when you need it, whether it be to signpost you to specific materials or offer book recommendations.

References and Bibliography

Berne, E. (1961) *Transactional analysis in psychotherapy.* Grove Press.

Department for Education (2014) *Promoting fundamental British values as part of SMSC in schools: Departmental advice for maintained schools.* Available at https://assets.publishing.service.gov.uk/media/5a758c9540f0b6397f35f469/SMSC_Guidance_Maintained_Schools.pdf (Accessed 26 January 2026).

Department for Education (2025) *Relationships education, relationships and sex education (RSE) and health education: Statutory guidance for governing bodies, proprietors, head teachers, principals, senior leadership teams, and teachers.* Available at https://assets.publishing.service.gov.uk/media/68b8499e11b4ded2da19fd92/Relationships_education__relationships_and_sex_education_and_health_education_-_statutory_guidance.pdf (Accessed 29 September 2025).

Flückiger, C., Del Re, A., Wampold, B. E. and Horvath, A. O. (2018) 'The alliance in adult psychotherapy: A meta-analytic synthesis', *Psychotherapy*, 55(4): 316–340. Available online https://psycnet.apa.org/fulltext/2018-23951-001.pdf (Accessed 9 September 2025).

Independent Schools Inspectorate (2025) *Handbook for the inspection of association independent schools, including residential (boarding) schools and early years settings.* Available at https://www.isi.net/site/uploads/1.02%20ISI%20Inspection%20Handbook%20September%202025.pdf (Accessed 26 January 2026).

McPhee, S. and Pugh, V. (2024) *Developing quality PSHE in secondary schools and colleges*. Bloomsbury.

Neufeld, G. and Maté, G. (2024) *Hold on to your kids: Why parents need to matter more than peers*. Vermilion.

Office for Health Improvement and Disparities (2022) *Working definition of trauma-informed practice*. Available at https://www.gov.uk/government/publications/working-definition-of-trauma-informed-practice/working-definition-of-trauma-informed-practice (Accessed 26 January 2026).

Ofsted (2025) *State-funded school inspection toolkit*. Available at https://assets.publishing.service.gov.uk/media/690b26c69456634d9795fde0/Schools_inspection_toolkit.pdf (Accessed 26 January 2026).

O'Shaughnessy, R., Berry, K., Dallos, R. and Bateson, K. (2023) *Attachment theory: The basics*. Routledge.

PSHE Association (n.d.) *Programme builders for PSHE education: Key stages 1–4 (secondary sample)*. Available at https://20248256.fs1.hubspotusercontent-na1.net/hubfs/20248256/Programme%20Builders/Secondary%20sample%20version.pdf?hsCtaTracking=e02faa43-0ba9-448d-82ce-ebbe1c6ccfad%7C098b7f32–04aa-401c-a7f1-b4e546839228 (Accessed 11 August 2025).

Public Health England (2014) *The link between pupil health and wellbeing and attainment: A briefing for head teachers, governors and staff in education settings*. Available at https://pshe-association.org.uk/hubfs/Vision/PHE%20briefing%20the%20link%20between%20pupil%20health%20and%20wellbeing%20and%20attainment.pdf?hsLang=en (Accessed 16 September 2025).

6 Developing the Child Within the Culture

Kelly Allchin

Leadership

Use form time to champion your tutees and be their in-house cheerleader. Leadership in schools can sometimes be seen in its formal sense, such as through school councils or head student roles, but it also develops more quietly through character. The form room is a great place to nurture this kind of leadership, and importantly, it should involve all students, not just those who put themselves forward for official positions. Young people often think about leadership in quite a narrow way, partly because they don't yet have the life experience we do. For many, being a leader means being 'the boss', the loudest in the room, or perhaps even the successful millionaire, but that misses all the subtle, day-to-day ways leadership shows up.

If you look at any group of people, leadership roles usually appear naturally. This isn't just true for businesses or organisations, but in everyday life too. You can even spot it in the youngest children. Watch a Reception class at play and you'll often see some pupils who are naturally looked up to by others. These children have never been near a boardroom, yet they already have a sense of who seems to be leading and why. They are also surprisingly good at spotting the qualities that make someone worth following (Stavans and Diesendruck, 2020). For us as tutors, the exciting challenge is to help pupils recognise that leadership isn't just about power or control, it's about influence, trust, and the values that inspire others to want to follow your example.

When developing leadership skills with your tutees, it's helpful to focus on the specific qualities that effective leaders often demonstrate,

DOI: 10.4324/9781003620976-7

such as oracy, problem solving, decision making, and integrity. Students need to understand that leaders don't have to bulldoze their way through situations; ethical, thoughtful leadership can be just as powerful, if not more so.

For example, imagine supporting a restorative conversation between one of your tutees and another student after an argument. If your tutee speaks honestly about what happened, answers questions thoughtfully, and shows a sense of morality by admitting mistakes and expressing genuine remorse, they are demonstrating integrity in action. With these conversations, continue to focus on the positives by using discussion prompts such as, 'Can you tell me about a time when you faced a similar challenge, but dealt with it differently?' Then use this as a springboard to focus on positive choices they could make in the future.

Or take a particularly taxing teaching day: If a pupil picks up on your verbal or non-verbal cues and checks in, or uses their sense of humour and quick-witted banter to lighten the mood, they are putting excellent oracy skills into practice. Moments like these might seem small, but they are concrete demonstrations of leadership qualities, showing that leadership isn't always about giving orders, it's about awareness, empathy, and using your skills to positively influence those around you.

As a collective, you could also consider the jobs that need doing in your form room as part of your daily or weekly **routines** that you have as part of your **6Rs**, and allocate these to students. This is common practice in primary schools but is often overlooked in secondaries, which is a shame, as it helps pupils develop responsibility and integrity. These tasks give pupils a real sense of purpose and responsibility while also demonstrating that leadership can be shown through consistent, everyday actions, not just big projects.

If you have a vertical tutor group, this opens up even more leadership opportunities. Older students can take on mentoring roles, supporting younger pupils as they settle into school or helping them navigate challenges in lessons and around the school. This can be as simple as giving guidance on homework routines, sharing advice about clubs or activities, or modelling positive behaviour in social spaces. Vertical groups also allow younger pupils to see leadership in action regularly, which can be inspiring and give them role models within their own form. Meanwhile, older students gain valuable experience in responsibility, empathy, and communication, further developing the character traits that underpin effective leadership.

The list of both practical and supportive jobs is endless. During form time, you'll constantly see your tutees making decisions on, for example, who takes on which task for Sports Day, and problem-solving, like working through a quiz or a form-time challenge. The **relationships** that you have with them, and the ones they build with each other, give you plenty of opportunities to notice moments of oracy, collaboration, and integrity. But do we always take the time to highlight these skills and link them back to leadership? For example, you might say, '7KA, I've just been listening to you discuss your fundraising ideas. The leadership qualities you've all shown are remarkable, you've been identifying and solving problems, making decisions together, and communicating effectively with one another. Well done!' Moments like this don't just celebrate effort; they explicitly help pupils connect everyday behaviours to the leadership qualities we want them to develop. Recognising these skills as they happen reinforces the idea that leadership is not just a title, but something everyone can practise every day.

Building Character and Values

Form time is a valuable chance to connect with your tutees and create space for conversations and activities that help them grow a strong sense of character. Of course, there will be times when your role is simply to share key information or deliver parts of PSHE or citizenship, but the real heart of form time is about guiding pupils to notice their positive qualities and think about the areas they might want to strengthen. When this happens, form time becomes more than just a routine part of the day, it turns into a purposeful opportunity to discuss, recognise, and practise the core values that build a positive sense of character.

The Character Education Framework Guidance (Department for Education, 2019) encourages schools to place character development at the heart of education, aiming to raise respectful, resilient, and responsible young people who contribute positively to society. It emphasises values such as respect, integrity, courage, self-discipline, and kindness, and advises schools to nurture these traits through a strong and consistent ethos, clear behavioural expectations, a curriculum that builds confidence and resilience, and meaningful opportunities both in and beyond the classroom. The guidance highlights that character education should not be treated as an optional extra but embedded across school life, with all pupils supported to develop into well-rounded individuals prepared for the challenges of adulthood. Form time lends itself perfectly to this: For young people, having an understanding of their ethos as a person can provide them with core values that can massively shape the decisions they make, the pathways they embark on, and ultimately, how to live their day-to-day life.

Often, schools jump straight into character and values work by asking big questions like, 'How do you show respect?' or, 'What could you do to be more resilient?' While some pupils can handle these, others may find them overwhelming. This is where form tutors can draw on familiar PSHE strategies, such as distancing techniques and peer support, which are especially helpful when exploring personal development in a safe and supportive way, something that Sophie-Lauren McPhee has outlined in Chapter 5: Teaching Personal, Social, Health and Economic Education (PSHEE).

With distancing techniques, this could involve creating mini case studies, watching short clips of teenage-based dramas, or even televised programmes about real-life schools, and asking pupils questions relating to these. This allows pupils to explore topics around character and values through stories or scenarios, rather than focusing directly on themselves. It creates a safe space for honest discussion, reduces embarrassment, and helps young people think critically about values and choices. A discussion based around, 'Why might Tommy be lashing out at his teachers like that?' or, 'If you were Tommy's best mate, what would you be saying to him?' will usually lead to much more open conversations than asking pupils, 'What do you need to do to better demonstrate respect in school?' because pupils can step into someone else's shoes, share their ideas more freely, and explore values without feeling like they're being put on the spot themselves.

Once you have built a safe space within form and your tutees have got to know each other a little better, some really lovely values and character work can take place through peer support. Ideally, we want young people to reach a point where they are more aware of their behaviour, how it impacts others, and how closely it matches the type of person they want to become. School is often a place where negative behaviour is spotted and sanctioned by adults; however, form time can offer something different, a chance for behaviour to be reflected on and unpicked alongside peers. Of course, this has to be done with care and sensitivity, but even exploring small, everyday issues together can be powerful. For example, you might raise something like, 'Some of our tutees may be struggling with homework and picking up lots of sanctions for not completing homework. Can anyone share any top tips?' Questions like this can spark really useful conversations, and often a piece of advice lands more effectively when it comes from a peer than from a teacher. Many times I've seen pupils repeat a point that a teacher has made, but when it comes from a fellow student, it suddenly seems to click and make sense. When this happens, it's a win-win: Those struggling get practical support, while those giving the advice are reinforcing their own skills, building empathy, and developing their sense of character at the same time. Over time, this kind of peer-to-peer work can create a real culture of shared responsibility and encouragement within the form.

Dealing With Sanctions

Form tutors are often tasked with speaking to their tutees about the sanctions they have received across the school. When done well, these conversations can be a really valuable chance for pupils to think about their choices, reflect on their behaviour, and develop their character. However let's be realistic, form time can often feel rushed, and discussions about sanctions can end up delivered almost like a script, with little real opportunity for honest reflection. A useful approach is to get your form group settled and working collaboratively as quickly as possible. This creates space in the week for pupils to complete tasks or discuss scenarios in small groups, giving you some precious time to have one-to-one conversations with those who might really need it.

It's important to separate the behaviour from the pupil. You're likely to receive a more positive and open response when it's clear you're addressing their actions rather than labeling them as 'bad' or 'naughty'. For example, instead of saying, 'You've been disruptive again', you might try, 'I noticed you received a couple of negative points in history. What happened in the lesson on Tuesday? Can we work out what led up to it and what we can learn from it?' Phrasing it this way makes it easier for pupils to open up about their behaviour instead of instantly going on the defensive. It also shows them that you want to listen, understand their point of view, and, most importantly, support them in learning from the situation.

Once the pupil feels safe, the conversation can become reflective. Asking simple, open-ended questions encourages them to think about what happened and why. Questions like, 'What was happening before this?' or, 'How do you think that affected other people?' help pupils step back and see the bigger picture. They begin to notice patterns in their behaviour and understand the effect their choices have on others. Pupils may argue about what they did, but exploring how it might have made others feel can open a more productive discussion. For example, 'You shouted at Mr Jones, why did you do that?' is action-focused and accusatory, whereas 'How might teachers feel when pupils get angry and shout?' encourages reflection and empathy. This isn't about letting them off the hook, the sanction is still valid, but your positive relationship that you have with the pupil can help unpick behaviour and highlight real-life consequences.

It's also really useful to link these conversations to character and values. Sanctions can easily feel like punishment for no reason, but if you highlight qualities they are developing, like responsibility, respect, or integrity, it becomes purposeful. You might say something like, 'It can be really hard to keep your cool when you're angry, and this isn't something that will happen overnight, but learning to control your emotions is a really useful skill. It will help people see the respectful side of your character'. Framing it this way helps pupils see the learning and growth side of the experience.

Keeping the conversation forward-looking is key. Don't dwell too much on what went wrong, they've often already had a telling off when the sanction was issued. Instead, focus on what can be done differently next time. Encourage pupils to think about how they can make things better or repair any harm, and make a point of noticing positive behaviour as soon as possible after the sanction. Something as simple as, 'I noticed you haven't received any more negative points in history, that's brilliant, well done' can keep the momentum going, reinforce progress, and show that their positive choices are being recognised too. Over time, these small but purposeful conversations help pupils link behaviour to personal growth and see sanctions as a chance to reflect and develop rather than just a punishment.

Promoting Personal Development Within the Form

Personal development in schools covers a huge range of areas, PSHE, citizenship, character education, careers guidance, and extra-curricular activities, to name just a few. For pupils, it can sometimes feel disjointed, as though all these elements exist in separate bubbles with little connection. They might sit in a lesson on wellbeing, then have a careers interview with the school's career advisor, followed by an afternoon assembly about school values, without necessarily seeing how they all link together. Form time can provide an opportunity to make these personal development connections explicit and to help pupils consider their growth more holistically.

In form, tutors have a chance to step back and have important conversations that pull these strands together. Discussions can explore how the skills learned in one area support success in another, for example, how resilience developed through PSHE or extra-curricular challenges can help in achieving academic goals, managing conflict, or navigating future career choices. Pupils can reflect on how the values they're encouraged to practise, such as respect, responsibility, and integrity, show up across different areas of school life, such as within lessons, clubs, interactions with peers, and school staff, but also how these can support them in making their place in society too.

In essence, form time becomes the velcro that links all of these areas together, forming strong connections to last a lifetime, and as tutees, you are the lucky people that get to witness this happening every day.

- Discuss with your form the qualities they look for in a leader or role model. Have them write these on post-it notes and collate them. Look for common themes and, as a form, decide on your top five or top ten qualities. Display these in your form room as your agreed leadership qualities and refer to them frequently when celebrating success or setting targets with your tutees. Over time, this helps pupils see and hear how they are demonstrating leadership in everyday actions, not just in formal roles. It also gives them a shared language to recognise leadership in themselves and their peers, which can encourage collaborative problem-solving and positive group dynamics.

- Build distancing techniques into form time to explore character and values safely. Create a slide deck with a different scenario on each slide and ask pupils to discuss in groups and come up with ideas. For example: 'Asif has noticed his friend is really stressed before exams, what could he do?' These take little time to prepare but spark lots of discussion. When observing your tutees' ideas, make sure to congratulate them and reference character traits specifically, such as 'That idea shows real empathy, Leo, fantastic contribution'. Another option is to have tutees prepare a short presentation about someone they admire, focusing on their character rather than achievements. This gives a snapshot of what they value and can feed into future conversations. For example, if a tutee admires Martin Luther King for his courage and integrity, you can consciously spot your tutee demonstrating those qualities and reward them, strengthening their character development.
- Consider how peer support could feature regularly in form time. This might involve keeping a values jar and asking tutees to nominate peers for positive actions; for example: 'Mia is always cheerful in the mornings', 'Blessing lent me a pen in science', or 'Theo did a great job as our football captain in PE.' This normalises celebrating the good and boosts self-worth. As the tutor, you can add your own nominations too, so all pupils hear lovely things about their character. Alternatively, set a weekly mission as a form group, simple actions like holding a door open, picking up litter, or checking in on someone who looks down. At the end of the week, pupils reflect on what they did and how it felt. Once well practised, missions can extend to their home or community, showing that character development supports all areas of life.
- Build weekly reflection slots into form time, where pupils work individually to think about an incident, positive or negative, using a pre-prepared worksheet or questions on the board. Encourage them to focus on what happened, how it may have affected others, and what they could do differently next time. At first, pupils reflecting on sanctions may write in

a defensive or action-focused way, but with regular practice and your support, they will gradually become more reflective and better able to show empathy for the impact their actions have on others.

- If possible, set aside specific days during form time where pupils can work collaboratively, while you hold short one-to-one check-ins with tutees. These may only last 3–5 minutes, but to the pupil, this is dedicated time where they have your full attention. Keep the conversations fairly open, asking how things are going and reflecting on what has gone well or what has been a challenge over the past week. When pupils know these one-to-one conversations will happen regularly, they often start to think about them in advance, mentally preparing for reflection. This further develops their skills in self-awareness and empathy, embedding a habit of thoughtful reflection over time.

References and Bibliography

Department for Education (2019) 'Character education framework guidance'. Available at https://assets.publishing.service.gov.uk/media/5f20087fe90e07456b18abfc/Character_Education_Framework_Guidance.pdf (Accessed 13 January 2026).

Stavans, M. and Diesendruck, G. (2021) 'Children hold leaders primarily responsible, not entitled', *Child Development*, 92(1), pp. 308–323.

7 Working with Others

James Nichols

Introduction

In every middle and senior leadership post that I held, I would say the same thing to form tutors: 'You have the most critical job in the school; you know our students best, and you are their first point of contact, but you do not work alone'.

As a tutor, you are a sole individual responsible for a group of students; however, you are also part of the bigger picture of that child's education and development. The role of the tutor, whilst acting as a vital individual, is also about collaboration with other colleagues. After all, every child is a jigsaw puzzle in which everyone that they encounter possesses a piece, or several pieces, that come together to show the whole picture. Whilst you might be the one who knows each student in your tutor group best and sees them on the most regular basis, your **relationships** with them will likely be different as a result. As such, you need, as a tutor, to be connected to the other stakeholders in that student's life who may hold other 'pieces' of the puzzle; who see and hear a different side to that student.

To be an effective tutor, you need to communicate and collaborate regularly with a plethora of colleagues, including Heads of Year, SENDCos, teaching assistants, pastoral leaders, parents/carers, and external agencies. You may be the one triangulating all the people involved in your tutees' education and development, ensuring that decisions are made in the best interest of every child. This can be challenging and conflicting at times; however, it can also be enriching. The best form tutors are those by whom the student knows they are truly 'seen'. Not only is there nowhere to hide for that student when

DOI: 10.4324/9781003620976-8

it comes to setting high expectations, but it also offers a relationship grounded in a deep understanding of who that student is, including their strengths and weaknesses, which fosters trust, celebration, openness, and support.

Conversely, those tutors who do not involve themselves in the child's school experience beyond their prescribed interactions, nor collaborate and communicate effectively with colleagues, are also noticed by students. These are the tutors whose **relationships** with students are transactional and superficial, confined to only registering them each day, and who, consequently, don't maximise the opportunities that being a tutor allows. Due to the lack of investment in terms of time, energy, and knowledge gained through collaboration with others, these students might have a form tutor, but they lack a champion – someone to hold them to account, someone to celebrate them and raise their self-esteem, and someone who knows them inside and out. These are the students who are often left to fend for themselves. Whilst those without immediate problems or needs may get along fine, even if not as well as their potential might allow, those who need these qualities in a tutor can be demonstrably undermined.

Whilst your interactions will not be confined to working just with those outlined in this chapter, we will explore your professional **relationships** with three crucial stakeholders: Heads of Year, SENDCos and parents/carers.

Head of Year (Pastoral Leads)

This will undoubtedly be your most regular and vital contact when it comes to your tutees. As a Head of Year, I found the step up from being a tutor to be challenging at first. Heads of Year, unlike tutors, do not focus on the day-to-day welfare of each student on an individual level. Instead, Heads of Year will be dealing with specific and limited instances of more complicated or challenging behaviour, issues that span the year group and matters related to attendance and statutory guidance. Their responsibility is the year group as a whole and the welfare of their tutor team. They will aim to ensure consistency of good practice across all tutor groups. Effective Heads of Year will hold regular meetings with their tutor team to share best practices and deploy strategies across tutor groups, ensuring a positive and shared experience for all students. You can maximise your relationship with your Head of Year in three key ways: Communication, proactiveness and collaboration.

First, communication. As a Head of Year, my pet peeve (and one that has carried over to all leadership roles) was being caught off guard by parents and carers or senior colleagues. Do not let the first time your Head of Year hears about a significant incident or a sudden change in a child be when that parent/carer rings the Head of Year in a bout of fury and rage, even when these emotions are entirely justified. Parents can, though thankfully very rarely, when upset, occasionally go above the tutor, and it is usually the Head of Year who has to calm them down, whether because they've been contacted directly or they have been signposted to them by the school receptionist or a member of the senior leadership team in the first instance. If the Head of Year is unaware of the situation, it becomes more difficult for them to support the parent. As a tutor, ensure that anything that could be sensitive or controversial, or that might escalate, is communicated to your Head of Year, even after inputting it onto your safeguarding platforms. Don't underestimate how many concerns your Head of Year will be reading. It's best to check, verbally or in writing, that they have seen it and give them the chance to ask follow-up questions. Even if you are handling it capably, consider dropping them an email or stopping by their office for a heads-up. As you get to know your tutees and their families, it will get easier to spot these potential landmines, but Heads of Year are removed from this and are reliant on your knowledge of these families. I used to have a rule that tutors should drop by once a day to share news, both good and bad, from their tutees. It was amazing how much a Head of Year can pick up from this. So, do them a favour, drop by regularly. Additionally, be sure to share the good stories as well. Not only do Heads of Year love to hear them, but it also means that they can drop this into their communications with parents and colleagues.

Second, be proactive (within reason) in managing issues whenever possible. Heads of Year will be eternally grateful to be informed of a problem which has a solution attached to it. This doesn't necessarily mean solving the issue yourself, but instead identifying the stakeholders who can resolve the matter and then monitoring their progress. If it's an academic issue, speak with the relevant colleagues.

If it's pastoral, then seek advice from the members of the wellbeing or pastoral team. Not only does this enhance your involvement with the student and your colleagues, but it is also a great way to develop the skills for whole-school impact. Just ensure that you document what you have done and/or share it with the Head of Year. Also, know your limits. If a problem is beyond your reach or expertise, ask for help from your Head of Year. Heads of Year, if they are genuinely supportive of their tutor team, will always prefer to mentor and support you in managing the situation rather than dealing with the fallout, which often includes not just the original issue but all of the problems that have piled up on top of it.

Third, collaborate and share good practice with your Head of Year. If you have designed a great tutor time activity, delivered a high-impact PSHE lesson, or participated in a CPD opportunity, please share any relevant resources or learning materials. As mentioned earlier, Heads of Year are concerned with ensuring consistency of excellence across their cohort. It can be problematic for Heads of Year, though it may feel good for the tutor, albeit selfishly, for one tutor group and one tutor to be obviously benefiting from academic or pastoral provision that others are not receiving. Being a student in a year group should not be a lottery, where your tutor group or tutor determines your success. If one tutor's group benefits from their practice, it can create an unfair advantage. Heads of Year will want and appreciate the opportunity to make opportunities available for their whole team. Of course, you should receive credit for your efforts, but you shouldn't seek one-upmanship on your tutor colleagues – it is only the students in the other groups who lose out. It is not a competition. Heads of Year might not be able to facilitate an exactly equal experience for your colleagues (after all, you can take horses to water, but you cannot make them drink). Still, they should have the chance to give the best provision for their tutees, even if it's not always utilised. Heads of Year will appreciate those colleagues who understand that. It also demonstrates that you are thinking like a pastoral leader of a cohort, not just your immediate group of students.

So, Heads of Year are a crucial relationship for you and your pupils. They should matter just as much as a Head of Department of your academic subject. The more you invest in that relationship, the better your tutees, your year group and your professional development will grow.

SEND Coordinator (SENDCo)

It is more than likely that at some point, one of your tutees will be a student with a special educational need or disability. This broad concept encompasses a wide range of physical, psychological and educational conditions which vary in severity and the level of provision required. As a form tutor, you can reach out to a student with SEND before they begin the term or year in your form group. Whilst all students are anxious, students with SEND will likely have additional feelings and concerns related to starting a new environment. In all of these, the SENDCo is a crucial colleague to interact with regularly. To be a form tutor who fully includes and celebrates every child's contribution and potential, there are three things incumbent on you as a form tutor working with your school's SEND Coordinator.

First, you need to understand the individual needs of students with EHCPs (Educational, Health and Care Plans), IEPs (Individual Education Plans) and Pupil Profiles. These will be distributed and updated regularly by the SENDCo. Form tutors must ensure that they have thoroughly reviewed these documents for all students in the form group, especially if the student is new to the school or has a newly established need, and implement any recommendations made for tutor times, assemblies, or peer-to-peer interactions. These plans will also be linked to your school's Individual Needs or SEND register, which the SENDCo will update. Ensure that, as a form tutor, you treat this as seriously as you would your classroom teaching. It is also good practice to make sure that you join meetings with the SENDCo to discuss progress towards the student's targets. Finally, the SENDCo will likely hold regular briefings and training sessions, as well as put training and development strategies in internal school communications. You should attend these sessions and ask any questions when you are unsure. The SENDCo will want to help and support you, though it is important to remember that their role is vast and complex. Being proactive and coming forward will be greatly appreciated.

Second, maintain consistent communication with the SENDCo and their team. Share observations about students' behaviour, progress and concerns. Whether this is done by formal email or even over coffee in the staffroom, SENDCos need to have a complete picture of all students with additional needs. Small changes in behaviour, progress or social interaction can be a vital sign that something needs addressing with these students, some of whom might struggle to articulate clearly that they need support. It is also crucial to communicate any concerns about emerging SEND needs in a student who has not yet been formally recognised. As a tutor, if you spot poor organisation (such as turning up late or not having the necessary equipment), anxiety, emotional changes, or academic struggles raised by subject teachers or the students themselves, it is essential to share this. Early identification of suspected SEND needs can enable assessment, and if appropriate, additional support to be put in place more quickly and effectively. As a tutor who sees every student the most regularly and frequently, this communication with the SENDCo is vital.

Third, get involved in the SEND needs and provision of your tutees. Your SENDCo can suggest numerous school-specific ways to do this. However, generally speaking, most SENDCos will encourage you not to be wary or afraid, but to be actively involved and informed in a student's SEND needs. This enables the fostering of a culture of empathy and respect towards neurodiversity, something that is not solely the responsibility of the SENDCo but of all staff members. Being proactive and positive with SEND students sets a role model for how other tutees in your form group should respond and engage with students with additional needs. You can also take practical action to make life more manageable for students with SEND: Have the teaching schedule of the day on the board, support emotional regulation through check-ins and promote opportunities for independence and success that are related to the strategies in the pupil's SEND profile.

SENDCos are some of the real heroes of a school. The difference and impact that they can make is extraordinary. However, they are exceptionally and increasingly busy in school environments, having to accomplish more with significantly less. As a form tutor, you can make a real difference to SEND students in your tutor group by fostering and maintaining extremely close and effective **relationships** with the SENDCo and their team.

Parents and Carers

The one central rule for working with parents and carers is always to remember that whilst they may not have the professional expertise that you possess, or they might not always communicate how they feel most productively, they (almost always) love their child and want the best for them, just like you. They obviously have an enormous stake in their child's development and education and know them best. When working with them it is essential to keep this in mind.

The most successful tutor– parent **relationships** that I have seen have always been those where communication is frequent, positive and collaborative. Ask yourself, how would you feel if the first time you spoke to your own child's tutor was to hear something negative? It sets the tone for the whole relationship. The best tutors always make sure to make contact very early on in the year or term to share positive stories about how the child has settled in and is doing well. This can be via phone calls, emails, a note in the planner or a comment at the school gate. Parents really appreciate that positive news, and it sets a positive tone for the relationship, which is helpful, especially if you need to discuss more challenging topics later on. There is a foundation of trust and mutual respect. The parent knows that you care. This can also make the family more open and willing to raise any concerns – whether academic, emotional, or about the family environment – that they have regarding their child with you, especially if the concerns are sensitive or uncomfortable. Similarly, you also need to ensure that your expectations are clear and that these are communicated to parents and carers who can help reinforce them at home. Taking the opportunity to praise when these are met, and to explain to parents and carers how and why they might not have been, is crucial for parents to buy into the triad relationship of school, home and student. Again, the more regularly this can be communicated and discussed, the stronger the trust and authority that you will have with the family. If this is something that you might find challenging, utilising the support of the Head of Year is a good first step.

Even with the best **relationships** between home and school, there might be times when, as a form tutor, you are in an uncomfortable discussion with a parent or guardian. The secondary school years are a turbulent time for students, and their parents might also be struggling to manage them. Viewing parents and carers as equals and acknowledging their experience and knowledge of the child is always essential. It is also important to maintain your professionalism by being calm, transparent and utilising the resources of the entire school community. You might not always be the best placed to help, but you have a vital role in signposting and securing the relevant support. In these cases, be transparent but also involved. If appropriate, follow up with the parents if they need to work with a colleague instead of you. Demonstrate that you remain interested and invested in resolving the situation or addressing the need by formally responding to communication within an appropriate time frame, usually set out by school policy.

Finally, remember that the child in school is not always the same as at home. As teachers, we can sometimes see personality traits, qualities, anxieties and changes that are not visible at home (and vice versa). Some children can be two sides of the same coin in their home and school settings. Quiet at home, but loud at school, smiling at home but looking anxious at school, doing reading in their lunch break, but constantly on the PlayStation at home. This really reinforces the need for regular and proactive communication. Of course, sometimes these differences can reflect concerns about safeguarding or wellbeing. If you suspect that something is not quite right, it is always important to register your concerns with the Designated Safeguarding Lead.

A great relationship with parents and carers is a real advantage to a form tutor. It means that your expectations will be reinforced and supported, allowing you to build a rich and comprehensive picture of the whole child in front of you. The parents will be forever grateful for your expertise and professionalism. As form tutors, we don't always realise the impact we have on both parents and children over time.

Being a form tutor is an amazing and rewarding role within a school. It really is the most critical job in the school. It is a chance to make a real difference. However, whilst there is a lot of responsibility, especially to do it as effectively as the students deserve, it is always important to remember that you are not working alone. You are a team, a school community. Everyone has pieces of the jigsaw. Working with others is not only essential for fully supporting every student, but it is also essential for your own support. It truly takes a village to raise a child.

- Ensure you have updated your Head of Year on how the tutor group is performing, including any key concerns and successes.
- Share any resources or activities that have worked well with your class with other form tutors.

- Check with the school's SENDCo about the students in your tutor group who have additional educational or healthcare needs, and how you can best support them.
- During the course of the half-term, please phone, email, drop a quick note, or speak to parents at the gates to introduce yourself and share one positive piece of good news about each of your tutees.

8 Key Stage 3 Tutoring

David Best

Transition and Changes

On the first day of the academic year, you look in front of you and see smiling faces full of excitement and anxiety. The changes that these 11 year-old pupils will then go through over the next three years will be both varied and drastic. You need to be prepared to adapt with those changes and nuance your approach to support them all throughout. As well as the academic transition into secondary school, pupils will also go through structural changes in adapting to a new school. They will also experience social and emotional transitions as their friendship groups change.

Pupils are faced with an environmental transition where secondary school settings are often larger than those of their primary schools. This can be overwhelming and even adults often find moving from one workplace to another challenging. These pupils may only have a few select friends from their previous school and face the possibility of being in separate form groups even if their friends have chosen to attend the same secondary school.

Research conducted by Jerrim and Kaye (2025) highlighted the major impact that a negative transition from a primary to secondary setting can have on pupil enjoyment and engagement following Year 7. A lack of support and guidance in the classroom can lead to future issues with behaviour and attendance. A form tutor is in prime position to alleviate this by establishing a positive and welcoming environment from the outset. Welcoming pupils as they enter the form room is such a strong tool that helps in establishing **routines** and through

DOI: 10.4324/9781003620976-9

consistency of this action you allow your tutees to view you as a **reliable** part of their school lives.

Stresses and Pressures

Secondary school settings place additional pressures on pupils, including an increased workload both in school and at home. Pupils are expected to develop their independence and can struggle with the expectations placed upon them in a new setting. Form tutors are at the forefront of establishing independent and resilient learners as you are well positioned to deal with any organisational problems before they become an issue. Through modelling early on the **rigour** with which your tutees should approach their studies you will enable them to flourish. Hopefully a PSHE-style subject will cover this, but a good starting point would be to introduce the topic of resilience and ensure that all students in the group are aware of what it means and how to call upon it. This can lead into a low stakes problem-solving question where there are events that will go wrong. For very new Year 7s, the big anxieties will be getting lost and encountering the older, bigger students. Work through their fears and thoughts with reassurance and rationality to ease these transition stresses.

Falling behind and subsequent feelings of becoming overwhelmed with the weight of expectations can place pupils in an uphill battle for the remainder of Key Stage 3 and even into Key Stage 4. If you're able to, tap into your experience of that change, or access reliable older pupils who can support in how they dealt with the stresses and pressures. This shows your form that you are **receptive** and understanding of the issues they face. At the end of the Key Stage in particular, Key Stage 3 pupils will go through the GCSE options process in preparation for their Key Stage 4 courses – the opportunity to listen and discuss with older and experienced students would be supportive for your tutees in giving them time to digest the opportunities ahead.

Wood et al. (2025) highlight the growing recognition of the importance of the mental and emotional health of pupils within secondary school education and the impact that the pandemic in 2020 had on accelerating these pressures on pupils. Your tutees are not only dealing with the transition in an educational setting but navigating the pressures of their own growing anxieties. These are exacerbated by the added workload and can often lead to pupils feeling overwhelmed. Pupils often lack the skills to handle these, and as form tutors we can support the development of the skills and resilience needed to handle these feelings. These anxieties are not only caused by school but may also be impacted by external factors such as family and experiences outside of school. Form time provides an opportunity to share some of these potential anxieties with your tutees so that they have a reference and can develop an understanding of some of the emotions and inner turmoil that they may be facing. Take time to help pupils create reminders or forward plan when to complete homework, for instance, so it is not always left until the last minute. Communicate with parents and carers, if allowed, or through the pastoral team so that they are kept in the loop.

The last 25 years have seen an awakening in our understanding of adolescent brain development and have moved us on from the initial belief that brains stop developing at the start of secondary school (Sawyer et al., 2018). Pupil transitions are various and ongoing throughout the Key Stages, and being able to comprehend the magnitude of the developments that their brains are going through at this time shows the value of the strategies that we are looking to put in place in order to support. This period of uncertainty and anxiety leaves pupils vulnerable to mental health problems (Blakemore, 2020). There is an increasing number of pupils facing socio-economic hardship and mental health problems post-pandemic, and a variety of strategies are important to support pupils through these. This puts form tutors on the front line and best placed to make a huge impact to support pupils pastorally so that they can adapt and grow, as well as continue to learn academically.

Throughout their time in Key Stage 3 the sensory and motor areas of the brain develop quicker during these years than the prefrontal cortex, which is continually developing throughout adolescence (Blakemore, 2020). This means that a lot of cognitive development is ongoing throughout Key Stage 3 and is still a long way from full completion at the end of this period. This is the area of the brain that impacts social and emotional understanding for pupils, as well as their decision making. It is only natural that this will leave pupils needing stability and reassurance throughout.

One of the barriers facing tutees is the fear of failure, and we need to be aware of our role in how we can reassure the students regarding this. Pupils often carry the burden of wanting to please parents and teachers by succeeding and this pressure can inhibit their interactions around school. It is important to model for pupils that it is fine to make mistakes and that learning takes place from those mistakes. Consider sharing something that went well for your week and something that did not go well. This gives the pupils a prompt to do the same, and you can look at the learning aspects of failure together and how useful it can be. This could be done as a group or quietly whilst the form is working on another activity.

Through my time in education, I have come to see that where some institutions focus on behaviour, others focus on culture within a school. This distinction is important, and as a form tutor I try to establish the right culture within my tutor group. I model punctuality and patience; I actively listen when they speak to me and I remind them of the same expectations. My opening form time discussion is always the difference between a reason and an excuse, and the importance of timing. A reason is given in advance, whereas an excuse is given afterwards. The other aspect I've found useful to model for Key Stage 3 is empathy for others. Understanding the position of others can be based on smaller examples such as falling outs between friends, or larger ideas of immigration and politics – schools can teach them the content, but as a tutor, I like to focus on the human side a lot more.

It may be a slow process at first but through a rigorous commitment to persevere with this activity then tutees will develop the skills to self-reflect and accept when things do not go well the first time around. It is important that when you try something with your form that you do not give up too quickly and allow the process to have a chance to have an impact. Otherwise, they will learn that by not engaging with an activity then the form tutor will just move onto something else. You want to set those high standards of engagement and lead by example. This also provides you with an opportunity to give **rewards** to those who are showing a desire to improve and engage in the class discussion, modelling what you are asking of the group.

Behaviour Expectations

You will notice a difference in how your Year 7 tutees behave compared with when they reach Year 9. Whilst we have spoken about the anxious

Year 7, your Year 9 tutees will be far more socially led in their choices. Their relationships with their friends and peers become more complex and intense. They will look to challenge authority and test the boundaries of the school community as they actively look to assert more independence. There will be an increase in volatility and risk taking, which will mean that it is vital to maintain the **routines** and continue being **receptive**. If you are new to the group in Year 9, I would offer one fundamental difference between Year 7s and 9s: Year 7s will most likely follow your instructions. Year 9s will most likely follow your instructions but want to know why they should. Some of my most fondest memories with teaching classes and form groups have been when they were in Year 9, especially if you've had them for the years beforehand.

Listening to your tutees is a vital aspect of the position and being **receptive** to their thoughts and feelings, especially when they get things wrong. How often have we heard a pupil say that they received a reprimand and it was not their fault? These can make for challenging conversations and negatively impact your relationship with your pupils if not handled skilfully. You are there to help your form whilst maintaining the sanctity of the behaviour policy and supporting colleagues. For example, a pupil has received a negative sanction for talking in a lesson: You speak with your tutee about this situation, and they claim that they 'turned around because they heard a noise but weren't talking'. A delicate situation can be handled with care by acknowledging how your tutee feels whilst providing them the opportunity to view the other side. I have regularly had conversations start with 'maybe ... but ...'. For instance: 'Maybe you were not talking this time, but you can appreciate how it may have looked when you were seen turning around' . By acknowledging the feelings of your pupil, you have somewhat defused the situation as you are not necessarily making a judgement on their words, but you are supporting your colleague and helping your tutee see the issue in a different light.

Values-based leadership is an important aspect of being a form tutor. Often schools will have their own way of expressing common values that are expected of pupils. It is important as form tutors that we model the merit of those values (Van Niekirk and Botha, 2017). Establishing **routines** and being **reliable** are core aspects of modelling these values to our tutees. They look to us for guidance and leadership. They will take cues for their behaviour from our own actions. Most schools' values will follow a common theme of uniform, punctuality and attitude towards learning, so we also need to look professional, arrive on time and with a positive, productive attitude.

First, by being at the door to greet pupils as they walk into form allows you to implicitly model punctuality and a positive attitude towards the school day. It also allows you to establish a positive rapport as they enter form time. This interaction sets up the rest of the form time as it has begun in a calm manner, and it also allows you an opportunity to pick up on any changes to your tutees in their emotions or energy levels.

Additionally, it allows you to discuss with them at various points the importance of turning up on time and that you are only expecting the same things that you are willing to do. This **rigour** allows you to lead your tutees by example and most will be inclined to follow. Enthusiasm is infectious, and by engaging with form time and showing that it matters to you, pupils will be more motivated towards the time they spend with you. This in turn sets them up with a stronger foundation for the school day or week ahead.

Ways You Can Support

A key aspect in coping with the transition for pupils is the importance of consistent **routines** and expectations. It is vital that these are established quickly and remain throughout the Key Stage 3 period. You can still make adaptations to these and should reflect on their effectiveness regularly; however, ensuring that the core message remains will provide pupils a source of comfort in a tumultuous time where many will be feeling a lack of control in the transitions that they are dealing with during this extended period of time. If your school or setting does not offer one, establishing a timetable of consistent form time activities so that pupils know what to expect throughout will help with this, and it can be a little generic such as reading, discussion, wellbeing, etc. This still gives you flexibility to adapt as necessary but pre-warn tutees of any upcoming changes, such as if an assembly has been moved to a different day. This is of particular benefit for some of your SEND pupils and often a school will have a system that you can utilise to provide announcements or take time to speak quietly with pupils who may be particularly negatively impacted by sudden upcoming changes. My current school itself utilises Microsoft Teams and has it embedded from Year 7, with pupils checking regularly for updates and sharing them with their peers.

Learning your tutees' names as quickly as possible and setting that challenge to yourself will make your form group feel more comfortable in school, particularly within your form room. The more important and valued pupils feel, the more comfortable they will feel, and it helps to establish yourself as a **reliable** part of their school life. Learning names is a powerful tool, and pupils pick up on the effort you have made to learn their names and use them. One anxiety facing tutees is that feeling of invisibility and that feeling that you do not have someone who cares about you at school. As educators we do care for our pupils and we want them to thrive. Getting to know their name helps them feel like they matter within the school and is a simple first step in establishing a greater rapport.

It is important to be 'present' throughout form time and engage with pupils. There will be times when you need to have difficult conversations with pupils, so it is essential to invest in your **relationships** with them early on. By engaging and getting to know your pupils, you establish a rapport early and accumulate some equity with them. Therefore, when you do need to have discussions about behaviour or attendance and you make a withdrawal from your rapport with the pupil, then you are still left with positive equity. This is better than the alternative, where you are left with negative equity that accumulates negative interest, and it is very difficult to turn those **relationships** around to reestablish positive rapport. Communicating with parents and carers about important updates through the planner or more directly is also beneficial. This is covered more in Chapter 7: Working With Others.

As a form tutor, you can utilise the form time environment to create a mini bubble with your form group. Engaging and getting to know the pupils, as well as helping them to integrate and support each other will benefit your pupils assimilating into the often larger secondary school setting and develop the confidence and resilience needed to thrive and contribute as they progress through their school life. An unexpected result of the pandemic is that the bubbles created as a safety measure have been found to aid the transition into secondary school (Cook, 2026). Facilitating and driving a camaraderie between your tutees can help establish support groups within the class and your tutees themselves will help to drive and generate an ever increasingly positive and welcoming environment.

Challenges Specific to Key Stage 3

Dealing with the social turmoil of making new friends or even maintaining prior friendships can pose challenges for pupils in settling into life at their new school. As a form tutor, we can support pupils with these **relationships** both old and new by utilising a dynamic seating plan for form time, which will help embed a strong and positive culture within your form group.

This facilitates a **receptive** environment for all and provides a good foundation for moving forward through the subsequent years. Getting to know your tutees in this way also allows you to support them around school by sharing with colleagues as you have a better idea of what motivates and comforts the pupils in your form. This should be an ongoing process too that is revisited regularly throughout the year as you get to know your form group and as your tutees grow in confidence. It provides your form an opportunity to share and the **rigour** of re-engaging in such conversations embeds skills that pupils need to solidify their peer **relationships** and further strengthen their trust in you. Often things that appear minor to us, such as sharing our favourite hobby, can mean a lot to children (Zheng, 2022).

As your form progresses into Year 8 they face fresh challenges, which can often include a loss of their love for learning or a decline in their own motivations. We can consider this as a second transition, where the decline in attendance and engagement is significant. Taking action to combat this as a form tutor can help your tutees deal with this before the problem accumulates through the subsequent years and really hinders pupils as they struggle to re-engage in Key Stage 4. This is where you should refer back to the **6Rs**.

In establishing set **routines** of expectations and building up **relationships** with your tutees, it makes it easier to spot any changes in engagement. Keeping on top of the school's behaviour record system, often in some form of **rewards** and sanction points, you can praise those doing well on a regular basis. This **rigour** shows your form group that you are maintaining an interest in how they are behaving and engaging in the school day, as well as providing you a positive opportunity to stress the importance of attendance.

A decline in motivation and engagement in Year 8 also coincides with an increase in workload and expectations. Pupils are expected to become increasingly independent in their learning as the challenge of the various curricula increases. This can cause a lot of strain on your tutees and can lead to a lot of additional behavioural issues around school and in form time. This in turn can lead to a decline in their confidence and resilience. This is where taking time to praise and reward the efforts of your form with regularity will be beneficial in both the short and longer term.

As external interests and distractions increase into Year 9, pupils often struggle to self-regulate and their anxiety increases. Their **relationships** with their peers become more complex and the changes of adolescence become more difficult for them to navigate. This is where establishing simple but consistent **routines** within form time provides pupils with a sense of reliability in what to expect, ensuring form time is a safe and familiar place for them to settle for the day ahead.

Year 9 often sees pupils face their first meaningful choices for their future with GCSE options. They are provided with a lot of information in a relatively short window and must make a choice on whether or not to continue with some subjects. This can be a daunting and overwhelming task. It is important that as their form tutor, you can not only reassure them but give them guidance or point them in the right direction to help make more informed choices. Use form time to share information, but also get pupils to discuss who they can speak to for advice. I would also recommend asking older pupils who study those subjects to come and offer a brief outline of what those subjects entail. Be sure to attune to the information and guidance given out by the school so that you do not contradict it. There are no 'easy' subjects, do not tell students to do or not do certain subjects, and talk through potential post-16 pathways and career ideas if you have the scope to. Some pupils may be making these choices under the weight of parents' biases and expectations, so it is vital that you are a neutral and encouraging voice to counteract this.

The time with your form group allows you some freedom to share and develop some of the transferrable skills that pupils will be developing throughout Key Stage 3 and that they will require to flourish at Key Stage 4. Take time to introduce effective study and revision methods and ways to work independently, actually modelling and discussing without the constraints of subject-specific curricula. You can make it an extra-curricular topic that the form group is interested in; for instance music-related. This can help you with difficult conversations later on when pupils may be struggling within certain subjects, and gives you a powerful reference point. Through **rewards** you can promote a positive mindset by encouraging pupils to persevere and give maximum effort.

Take the time to show pupils the benefits of looking after their mental health and being able to unwind. The bonds that you establish with and between your tutees in Key Stage 3 set the foundations for successfully managing the rigours of Key Stage 4.

- Get to know your tutees' names as quickly as possible and use them regularly.
- Share a skill associated with life in school with your tutees and encourage them to focus on it for the week, such as doing a nice deed or learning the name of someone from another form.
- Set a few simple expectations as part of the routine and give it time to embed, in particular being at the door for the start of form time.

References and Bibliography

Blakemore, S-J. (2020) *Neuroscience, adolescence and GCSEs: A misalignment?* Available at https://rethinkingassessment.com/rethinking-blogs/neuroscience-adolescence-and-gcses-a-misalignment/ (Accessed 28 August 2025).

Cara, N. (2022) *What is the nature and value of the Form Tutor and Form Time in secondary schools in England? What happens, how does it happen and why is it important?* Available at https://discovery.ucl.ac.uk/id/eprint/10152217/ (Accessed 1 February 2026).

Cook, V. (2026) *The transition from primary to secondary school: Recommendations from research.* Available at https://my.chartered.college/research-hub/the-transition-from-primary-to-secondary-school-recommendations-from-research/ (Accessed 1 February 2026).

Harris, M. and Johnston, M. A. (2009) 'Values-based leadership: At the heart of sustaining school reform and improvement', in S. Huber (ed.), *School leadership: International perspectives.* pp. 145–158. Springer.

Hinze, V., Montero-Marin, J., Blakemore, S. J., Byford, S., Dalgleish, T., Degli Esposti, M., Greenberg, M. T., Jones, B. G., Slaghekke, Y., Ukoumunne, O. C. and Viner, R. M. (2024) 'Student-and school-level factors associated with mental health and well-being in early adolescence', *Journal of the American Academy of Child and Adolescent Psychiatry*, 63(2), pp. 266–282.

Jerrim, J. (2025) *Mind the engagement gap: A national study of pupil engagement in England's schools.* Available at https://www.impactedgroup.uk/resources/report-mind-the-engagement-gap (Accessed 1 February 2026).

Jerrim, J. and Kaye, N. (2025) *The decline in pupils' emotional engagement with school. How does England compare to other countries?* Available at https://repec-cepeo.ucl.ac.uk/cepeow/cepeowp25-03.pdf (Accessed 1 February 2026).

Sawyer, S. M., Azzopardi, P. S., Wickremarathne, D. and Patton, G. C. (2018) 'The age of adolescence', *The Lancet Child & Adolescent Health*, 2(3), pp. 223–228.

Stiebahl, S. and Lally, C. (2024) *Mental health support for young people in schools.* Available at: https://doi.org/10.58248/HS83 (Accessed 1 February 2026).

Titchmarsh, A. (2019) 'Role of the form tutor', in S. Capel, J. Lawrence, M. Leask and S. Younie (ed.) *Surviving and thriving in the secondary school.* pp. 58–68. Routledge.

Van Niekerk, M. and Botha, J. (2017) 'Value-based leadership approach: A way for principals to revive the value of values in schools', *Educational Research and Reviews*, 12(3), pp. 133–142.

Van Rens, M., Haelermans, C., Groot, W. and Maassen van den Brink, H. (2017) 'Facilitating a successful transition to secondary school: (How) does it work? A systematic literature review', *Adolescent Research Review*, 3, pp. 43–56. Available at https://doi.org/10.1007/s40894-017-0063-2 (Accessed 1 February 2026).

Wood, M., Pennington, A., Su, F., Laver-Fawcett, A., Gabriel, L. and Sinani, C. (2025) 'The ongoing impact of the COVID-19 pandemic on adolescents' (11–18 years) mental health and wellbeing in the UK: A scoping review', *Pastoral Care in Education*, pp. 1–21.

Zheng, F. (2022) 'Fostering students' well-being: The mediating role of teacher interpersonal behavior and student–teacher relationships', *Frontiers in Psychology*, 12. Available at: https://www.frontiersin.org/journals/psychology/articles/10.3389/fpsyg.2021.796728/full (Accessed 1 February 2026).

9 Key Stage 4 Tutoring

Andy Allman

Introduction

The much peddled Stanford Duck Syndrome (Açkay and Ohashi, 2024) – where the calmness of a duck on a pond is juxtaposed with the ferocity of the legs under the water – is something I think about often when working with Key Stage 4 tutor groups. The calm kids may not be calm. The organised kids may be panicking. The laid-back kids may be stressed. What's more is that the metaphorical duck may have a terrifyingly high number of legs kicking and thrashing: Social pressures, future plans, revision, workload, homework, relationships, friendships, identity, rebellion – so how does one tutor manage all these issues?

Well first, they can't – Chapter 7: Working With Others focuses explicitly on working with others and this should be remembered. A good tutor uses staff and resources at their disposal – they are not a one-person pastoral Batman, taking on all issues. Chapter 2: Wellbeing and Safeguarding and Chapter 3: Attendance and Punctuality provide illustrative measures on maximising what you can accomplish as a tutor and should also be cross-referenced.

So, let's start putting our ducks in a row, shall we?

Transition and Change

Note: When writing this, I had the traditional three-year Key Stage 3 (KS3) and two-year Key Stage 4 (KS4) in mind, but to be honest, much of the advice and guidance here will work regardless of a school's curriculum model.

 DOI: 10.4324/9781003620976-10

The first half term of Year 10 is usually akin to a honeymoon phase. There is a novelty of students having ownership over their lessons. Often they notice that they are treated with some more maturity by staff. This will fade once the workload and assessments kick in and the novelty of that first September will be over.

You'll see this on plenty of schools' homework policies: That the expected frequency and length of homework increases at KS4 and often this work is greater in importance as it may mean the difference between finishing a topic or not. The school and staff will often expect KS4 students – implicitly or explicitly – to be the standard bearers for the younger years, so expectations of maturity and behaviour increase. At the same time, stress levels at this time will most likely also hit levels not seen by the students before. Assessments, applications, examinations – it's covered more later on but the jump for the students between KS3 and KS4 is significant.

Now, many people would be aware of the many stereotypes associated with young people, however unfair these stereotypes may be. Some stereotypes, however, are born in the midst of truths. The development of the adolescent brain typically brings with it emotional outbursts, increased risk taking, and a more finely tuned sense towards the importance of social acceptance amongst their peers (Griffin, 2017). All of this (and more) will see pretty clear changes from the beginning of Year 10 compared to when a form group will sit their GCSEs at the end of Year 11.

The change in personalities within your form group – and the overall personality of the form group – is to be fully expected, but this brings a change in prioritisation for the tutees. Chien et al. (2011) explained how the mere presence of peers can impact an adolescent brain to engage in riskier behaviours, which in a school setting could result in disruption, rebellion and disengagement. So what can a form tutor do against a naturally occurring hormonal shift? This may sound simplistic, but take into account some the **6Rs** – particularly **rigour** and **receptive.**

If the shift in personalities brings with it attitude and disruption, a rigorous approach to your form group means that seating plans have been adjusted, or that the resource for the morning session has been prepared ahead of time, potentially shutting down hopes of opportunistic nonsense from students looking to impress one another. Friendship shifts and rifts, and students looking for the low-hanging fruit of social conformity, will also play a role in the shifting sands of adolescent personalities. It should also be said that some personalities will not change that much – just becoming different versions of themselves over time.

The absolute beauty of being a form tutor is that each form is its own small community. There are quirks, cliques and personalities within the group that add to its collective persona. To make the most out of your group, this point is quite straightforward. Be as **receptive**, as welcoming, as interested as possible in these shifting quirks and evolving personalities. The students make the form – you are there to lead and to guide them. Be **receptive** to it. Dynamics within your group and school will inevitably change over time. Students may come and go, pressures and priorities will change as the students get older, so don't discount this – be open to it, almost expectant, and your students will appreciate that steady hand especially towards the business end of KS4.

If you are part of a Vertical Tutoring (VT) system at your setting, these changes (and stresses, pressures, etc.) will still be evident. There may be a higher emphasis on leadership and mentoring within VT (Chapter 6: Developing the Child Within the Culture examines this in more detail), but for the individuals involved their teenage brain, emotions and experiences will be comparable to other KS4 students in other settings. You may need to give them suitable amounts of space and flexibility in order to support them as you need to, but as ever, consult your Pastoral Leads for advice and guidance.

Stresses and Pressures

This section could have been placed within the 'Specific Challenges' section, but it is worth extrapolating and examining both as separate bodies. However, do try to join the two together when looking at your tutor group as a whole. We should not dismiss stress as merely a lazily attributed symptom of the post-Covid world. Stress amongst teenagers has been rising since the start of the 20th century (Hartas and Kuscuoglu, 2020) with socio-economic factors as a main cause, but also gender. Girls were found to have lower emotional wellbeing than boys, and this mirrors my anecdotal professional experience. Not all students will stress equally, and not all stresses will manifest equally: It may appear as acting out in lessons, snappy responses, or high levels of anxiety.

A common denominator of any KS4 student is the fact that they experience, many for the first time, what it takes for them to pass qualifications: Coursework, revision and examinations. I had a Year 11 form when I worked in a Pupil Referral Unit (PRU), I have had a form in a state comprehensive and I have been Head of Year 11. For the most part, students have the same desire to do well, as they know (and are told repeatedly) that they need specific things to open doors to the next stage of their life. We live in an age where many people try to protect young people from stress. These intentions are good, but can be misguided. Stress can be good, it can be useful, if harnessed properly, and be used to good effect (Dhabhar, 2012). Students may respond more productively when the stakes are seen to be higher, or when their chosen post-16 destination may be on the line. There's then the argument about being able to handle stress positively in later life, so clearly we don't want to shield students from all stress. We should instead protect young people from unnecessary or additional stresses that may make their stress buckets overflow. We can coach students to understand that by completing homework, bringing the right equipment, organising their time, etc., they can minimise additional stresses such as sanctions and conflicts with staff. Patience and understanding with them is a must: It may be a case of overcoming obstacles, or letting them make their own mistakes, before solutions become embedded.

When I sense a group has rising stress levels, I look at the **reliable** aspect of the **6Rs** and make sure that I will know more than they do about what's happening. Venues, timings, equipment, expectations – this becomes easier the longer you teach, but it really helps reassure the students. At this point I also regularly talk about managing stress. In short, examinations are something that they cannot control – they are happening irrespective of what they do. They *can* control the level of preparedness for these examinations. Students can control their day-to-day level of stress by cooperating with staff about uniform, homework, punctuality, so that conflict is avoided or minimised. You can't remove the stress, but you can coach them around the nuances of stressful situations. Be wary here of the development of the adolescent brain, with the National Institute of Mental Health (2023) explaining that not only is the teenage brain more susceptible to stress, but it will also react differently to stress compared to an adult brain. A teenage brain is able to be coached through stress (National Institute of Mental Health (2023), and Putwain et al. (2023) found that specific exercises help teenagers more effectively in times of stress, such as breathing exercises, mindfulness, guided visualisation, so it may be worth reading up on these and signposting students to these types of resources (please note: Do not 'teach' students these exercises unless you are professionally qualified to do so; it is beyond the role and responsibilities of a teacher).

Some stresses link back to the previous sections on burgeoning personalities, so conformity, friendships and relationships can play an awfully important role. Usually, the crux of these stresses tend to be acute, and with a positive working relationship with a student (and those around them) these can be carefully managed through discreet conversations. I've found openers like 'Is this a home thing, a school thing or a friend thing?', or 'I've noticed that you're quieter in form than usual, you're struggling with organisation and you seem to be more distracted?' to be successful in allowing students to express themselves. Similarly, ensure that your conversations and phrasing focuses on the positive, such as, 'If you work hard you will get what you need', rather than, 'If you don't work hard then you won't get what you need' . Just remember to record any safeguarding and wellbeing concerns according to your school policy.

For helping students deal with stress, please do check through Chapter 7: Working with Others – it offers great insight into how to work with other professionals and stakeholders, who may be able to give you more background information or insights and allow you to help students on a daily basis. This is especially useful for stresses that are external to school – stresses that students bring into the building, such as care placements, family illness, etc. They say a village raises a child, but it takes a whole staffroom to get them through compulsory education.

And we can't really talk about stresses and pressures without coming back to what the mental health charity Place2Be says is the biggest stressor for teenagers: Exams and grades (BBC, 2024). For this, you will be a vital cog on a very structured and rigorous wheel: Mock examinations, coursework deadlines, intervention sessions – all of these will be managed by other staff members, usually Pastoral Leads or members of Senior Management. If you've had the group for many years by this point, you will become every stereotypical role that a government 'Get Into Teaching' advert can muster. Sometimes all at the same time. But even if you've only known the group for a few months, stay on top of the dates, get a sense of whether your group needs to be pushed or pulled and again, work with key stakeholders (especially parents/carers) and communicate concerns or dates. At this point in their academic journey, you need to be the smartest person in the room – it will offer reassurances and a sense of calm.

Expectations of Behaviour

It is no secret that positive relationships go hand-in-hand with more positive behaviour. Martinez and Wighting (2023) demonstrated that positive student– teacher relationships reduce disruption, whilst Obsuth et al. (2016) found that the positive impact of these relationships can last for years after the initial interaction. Elhaggagi (2009) wrote about the direct link between the form tutor and the improvement of student attendance, so it is no surprise, then, that we find ourselves coming back to the **relationships** strand of the **6Rs** for this section.

I mentioned this in the introduction but I'll reiterate it again: One cannot prioritise building relationships over other professional responsibilities such as pedagogy or safeguarding. If staff consistently shout at students or classes, or belittle colleagues or the school, then the outcome tends to be students adopting similar strategies, resulting in a negative climate for the class. Please do not mistake being liked by students for a positive student– staff relationship. A positive relationship will have clear evidence of transparency, consistency, and boundaries and may be built over time rather than instantaneously.

The varying contexts in terms of tutors who take on KS4 form groups are plentiful. Has the tutor had them previously as a tutor or as a teacher? Is the teacher new to the school? Is the teacher experienced in the school but new to the group? Is the teacher new to the school entirely – and what is the whole school culture towards new staff? How many tutors has the group had previously and how impactful has tutor time been? It is hard to quantify exactly, but do be aware that their experience of tutor time prior to you may play into what to expect from some of the attitudes and behaviour. Sethi and Scales (2020) found correlations between teacher– student **relationships** towards the motivation of students, and of student positivity towards school, so arguably this is a crucial part of the role to get right. There are hundreds of great articles and books specifically on behaviour management and also on body language, so don't be afraid to read up on areas that would benefit you and your students.

One of my most-used pieces of advice that ought to be fundamentally enshrined into the role is that tutor time should be handled like lesson time, with the same expectations, **routines** and, importantly in this case, behaviour systems. Just because it's tutor time does not mean that students are exempt from expectations or consequences. This, by the way, works both ways: **Rewards** in tutor time should be as frequent and as celebrated as they would be in a lesson. So be sure to know your school systems and to use your school systems if necessary.

Ways to Support Your Form Group

The most tangible way a form tutor can help address the jump between KS3 and KS4 workload is a gentle barrage of organisational support. Students will need to understand that they do not have to leave GCSE homework until the last minute, how to use out of school time effectively and how to plan throughout the week. If you have known the group since KS3, knowing the commitments of the students can really help, as comments such as 'I have football/LAMDA/cycling tonight' will be bandied about as a way for students to attempt to excuse themselves from their obligations. You will find yourself nagging at students, reminding them of the need for organisation, and encouraging them to speak to subject teachers if there are genuine issues regarding work. The use of school planners – or other recording systems like online platforms – can usually be monumental to some students, especially in the early stages. Online or paper copies of weekly plans can be shown, discussed, worked through, and even filled in on behalf of certain students in need of the most support, before introducing students to more nuanced concepts such as timeboxing (Zao-Sanders, 2018). With previous groups I have found it useful to draw a timeline of Year 10, Year 11, or the term, or the entire Key Stage, and map out for them key events but also when stress levels may rise. I found that the combination of the visualisation and the wider context of their journey helped students to break down the spectre of this stage of their education.

But in truth, it's not as easy as throwing planners and grids at them. A large part of getting this part of the role down will be explaining the need for greater ownership and maturity on their part, which comes through the coaching element of the **relationships** strand of the **6Rs**, and the **reliable** strand will have to be utilised in order to ensure these standards and expectations are consistently met.

Some of the most productive ways that a tutor can support their group during KS4 can be found in Chapter 1: Knowing Who's in Your Form, and Chapter 7: Working With Others. By understanding your group, you'll be able to understand who else should be involved in supporting them. This could be as little as knowing which students are into sport or animals, and working with a Careers Lead to familiarise yourself with suitable post-16 courses. It could be knowing which student may have a more complicated home life, so may need extra equipment or organisation when it comes to mock examinations. As a tutor, you may find yourself as the mortar between bricks – holding things together to stop things from tumbling down. Working with other professionals and colleagues will also ensure that greater pastoral support can be in place if required, which may be amplified at times of stress such as coursework deadlines, examinations or applications.

For when it comes to the crucial time of post-16 applications, there are some very simple and high impact things that you as a tutor can do. First, have at least a basic working knowledge of local providers and different types of qualifications so you are able to engage in conversations with individuals and the group. Support dialogue and meetings with the school Careers Lead. Ensure engagement with any assemblies or activities in tutor time are as high as they can be. Contact parents/carers, pastoral or school career advisors if you have concerns or questions about students. Also, try to be aware of any application deadlines and open evenings that your students may want to be aware of. Your job will be to gently push – the students must make their own decisions, but some support and advice may be welcomed. During KS4, an adolescent brain may develop the ability of long-term thinking (Allen and Waterman, 2024) but this can take up until they are 17 years old, so applying to college or sixth form as a 15 year-old will be more difficult for some as they simply can't get their heads around the need to think about the future.

If you can afford to do so, consider using some of your non-teaching time to either arrange a time, or to drop in or meet with members of your form (it is worth checking with the teaching staff first). It may be a wellbeing conversation, or support with an application, but they'll do better knowing that you're there to help. And remember to relay any concerns to the relevant system or professional within your setting.

Specific Challenges

Part of having a KS4 form group is that they will inevitably be faced with deciding what to do after their GCSEs. Depending on your school, you may have significant engagement with this process or more of an unofficial 'overseer' role, but it's worth thinking about a few key points. The first is that some students may become very stressed over the post-16 conundrum. What type of course? Which subject(s)? Do I stay here or go elsewhere? Not to mention the potential fear and anxiety of leaving somewhere that they've known for many years. These applications also generally come after a period of mock examinations, so you won't find students at their most relaxed.

Something that crops up over the course of KS4 is the prospect of students engaging in part-time work. Despite the numbers of teenagers having a part time job being in decline (Gardiner, 2020), it is estimated that still around a quarter of students will have some sort of paid work, not including any volunteering or work-based experiences. Your role here is to promote the concept of responsibility. Yes, we do want young people today to have financial independence and gain workplace skills, but ideally not at the expense of academic qualifications. Ensure that they know their rights such as hours of work permitted on a school night or on weekends. Ensure that it does not impact homework, revision or attendance. And ensure that if you have any concerns, to communicate these to the proper channels such as Pastoral Leads or parents/carers. The development of the teenage brain and the search for a social identity tend to lead teenagers into certain behaviours, one of which manifests as a desire for independence as their search for an identity progresses (Swzedo et al., 2017). Similar to the problems that a tutor may face when encouraging students into post-16 options, if we push back too hard on part-time jobs, tutors may run the risk of getting nowhere. Instead, carefully offer support, guidance and reminders of the entire spectrum of the students' responsibilities to ensure that one does not negatively impact another.

If we also remember the sections on exam and assessment-based stress, the challenges presented to a KS4 group are not insignificant.

When we combine these challenges, things can become overwhelming. All it may take is a fall-out over Snapchat, a bad shift at work, or a lower-than-expected mark and in the mind of a young person the world may have ended. For all this, however, the students at this age can be the most hilarious, thought-provoking and enjoyable to be around. If you have a tutor group from Year 7 all the way through to Year 11, that is around 900 form times that you will have shared with them – and they'll never forget that.

- I repeat this so often that I may make it a bumper sticker for my car, but treat your tutor time like a lesson. Expectations, seating plans, routines, consequences. There may be some wiggle room in some of this, with some groups, some of the time, but these should be very much the exception rather than the norm.
- Be the person in the know, or know who is. When it comes to exam dates, or entry requirements, or what Maths paper is calculator or non-calculator, know what they'll need to be told because often they'll ask you first. If you don't know the answer to something, don't guess – know the people within the school who the students can go and find the answer from.
- Use parents/carers as a positive outlet right from the get-go. Give them insights to how well their child is doing, if you've noticed any changes, if you're particularly proud or concerned regarding something in particular.
- Similarly, offer the parents/carers updates on how the group are doing – upcoming dates, shift in attitudes, deadlines, etc. If you send a group email to parents and carers, be sure to use the 'bcc' function to keep all email addresses private. I used to bookend half-terms with things to look out for – I found that parents/carers of only children or eldest siblings that had not been through the system before were particularly grateful.

References and Bibliography

Akçay, E. and Ohashi, R. (2024) 'The floating duck syndrome: Biased social learning leads to effort–reward imbalances', *Evolutionary Human Sciences*, 6, pp. 1–16. Available at: https://doi.org/10.1017/ehs.2024.20 (Accessed 30 January 2026).

Allen, B. and Waterman, H. (2024), 'Stages of adolescence'. Available at: https://www.healthychildren.org/English/ages-stages/teen/Pages/Stages-of-Adolescence.aspx (Accessed 30 January 2026).

BBC (2024) 'Children's Mental Health Week: Exams the biggest worry for school children says Place2Be'. Available at: https://www.bbc.co.uk/newsround/68165319 (Accessed 30 January 2026).

Chein, J., Albert, D., O'Brien, L. Uckert, K. and Steinberg, L. (2010) 'Peers increase adolescent risk taking by enhancing activity in the brain's reward circuitry', *Developmental Science*, 14(2), pp. F1–F10. Available at: https://doi.org/10.1111/j.1467-7687.2010.01035.x (Accessed 30 January 2026).

Dhabhar, F. (2012) 'Good stress, bad stress'. Available at: https://med.stanford.edu/news/all-news/2012/12/good-stress-bad-stress.html (Accessed 30 January 2026).

Elhaggagi, C. E. (2009) 'Secondary school attendance: The role of the form tutor: An autobiographical inquiry'. Available at: https://eprints.soton.ac.uk/73332/ (Accessed 30 January 2026).

Gardiner, L. (2020) 'Never ever: Exploring the increase in people who've never had a paid job'. Available at: https://www.resolutionfoundation.org/app/uploads/2020/01/Never-ever.pdf (Accessed 30 January 2026).

Gov.uk (n.d.) 'Child employment'. Available at: https://www.gov.uk/child-employment (Accessed 30 January 2026).

Griffin, A. (2017) 'Adolescent neurological development and implications for health and well-being', *Healthcare*, 5(4), p. 62. Available at: https://doi.org/10.3390/healthcare5040062 (Accessed 30 January 2026).

Hartas, D. and Kuscuoglu, A. (2020) 'Teenage social behaviour and emotional well-being: The role of gender and socio-economic factors', *British Journal of Special Education*, 47(3), pp. 329–349. Available at https://doi.org/10.1111/1467-8578.12328 (Accessed 31 January 2026).

Martinez, R. and Wighting, M. (2023) 'Teacher–student relationships: Impact of positive behavioral interventions and supports', *Athens Journal of Education*, 10(3), pp. 397–410. Available at: https://files.eric.ed.gov/fulltext/EJ1399789.pdf (Accessed 31 January 2026).

National Institute of Mental Health (2023) 'The teen brain: 7 things to know'. Available at: https://www.nimh.nih.gov/health/publications/the-teen-brain-7-things-to-know (Accessed 31 January 2026).

Obsuth et al. (2016), 'A non-bipartite propensity score analysis of the effects of teacher–student relationships on adolescent problem and prosocial behavior', *Journal of Youth and Adolescence*, 46, pp. 1661–1687. Available at https://doi.org/10.1007/s10964-016-0534-y (Accessed 31 January 2026).

Putwain, D., Chamberlain, S., Daly, A. and Sadreddini, S. (2014) 'Reducing test anxiety among school-aged adolescents: A field experiment', *Educational Psychology in Practice*, 30(4), pp. 420–440. Available at https://doi.org/10.1080/02667363.2014.964392 (Accessed 31 January 2026).

Sethi, J. and Scales, P. C. (2020) 'Developmental relationships and school success: How teachers, parents, and friends affect educational outcomes and what actions students say matter most', *Contemporary Educational Psychology*, 63. Available at https://doi.org/10.1016/j.cedpsych.2020.101904 (Accessed 31 January 2026).

Szwedo, D. E., Hessel, E. T., Loeb, E. L., Hafen, C. A. and Allen, J. P. (2017) 'Adolescent support seeking as a path to adult functional independence', *Developmental Psychology*, 53(5), pp. 949–961. Available at https://doi.org/10.1037/dev0000277 (Accessed 31 January 2026).

Zao-Sanders, M. (2018) 'How timeboxing works and why it will make you more productive'. Available at https://hbr.org/2018/12/how-timeboxing-works-and-why-it-will-make-you-more-productive (Accessed 31 January 2026).

10 Key Stage 5 Tutoring

Kim Constable

Transition and Change

The transition from Key Stage 4 to Key Stage 5 is a substantial and often underestimated shift in a student's experience. While the academic demands of post-16 education are significant, the deeper challenge lies in the wider transformation expected of learners. Students must quickly adopt new levels of independence, self-discipline and emotional resilience, expectations that can feel overwhelming without adequate preparation or support.

A common but flawed assumption is that students arrive in Year 12 suddenly more mature or autonomous simply because they have chosen to continue into sixth form. In reality, they are only around two months older than they were at the end of Year 11, with no meaningful developmental leap in maturity or executive function (Taverner et al., 2001; Shinwell and Defeyter, 2017). Yet from day one, they are often treated as if they have already become young adults, without any transitional period to help them develop these attitudes or behaviours.

This mismatch between expectation and readiness has important implications for the form tutor. Sixth form students enter an environment where the freedoms of post-16 study – relaxed or no uniform, independent study periods, fewer structured lessons – sit alongside the expectation of adult-like responsibility. As a result, they are far more likely than younger students to question **routines**, challenge boundaries, or push back against systems they perceive as overly restrictive or insufficiently justified. They see themselves as older, more independent, and therefore expect to be treated with a greater level of agency.

DOI: 10.4324/9781003620976-11

For this reason, the way a Key Stage 5 tutor builds **relationships** must differ from the approach used in Key Stage 3 and 4. Younger students tend to accept **routines** because 'that's just how school works' . Sixth-formers, however, respond best when tutors do not simply set boundaries, but clearly articulate the purpose behind them. Explaining why structures exist, why punctuality matters, why tutor time is purposeful, why deadlines are non-negotiable, and the expectation around communication with their teachers, helps students understand that expectations are not arbitrary but are designed to support their academic success and wellbeing. This approach fosters **relationships** built on mutual respect: Students feel they are being treated as emerging adults, and tutors demonstrate trust in their capacity to engage with reasoning, not just rules.

Research on summer learning loss also highlights that many students start Year 12 having lost academic **routines** and confidence (Shinwell and Defeyter, 2017). They are then faced with Level 3 curricula that demand independent study and conceptual depth, often without the scaffolding they relied on during GCSEs. Taverner et al. (2001) note that this academic and emotional adjustment can generate anxiety, which may motivate engagement but can also feel destabilising without support.

Here, the form tutor becomes a crucial stabilising presence. As the consistent adult in students' daily **routines**, the tutor can reinforce expectations calmly and explain why they matter. Tutor time provides an essential space to help students understand that these expectations support their development, independence and success.

Tutors also guide students in reconceptualising learning itself. Independent study is not simply more homework, it is a shift in mindset. Many students enter sixth form still operating with GCSE-style habits and limited awareness of the self-directed nature of Level 3 work (Thompson, 2021). Success requires students to reshape their beliefs about learning and engage more deeply. This aligns with guidance that self-regulation and metacognition must be explicitly taught and scaffolded, especially during transitions (Education Endowment Foundation, 2025a). Higher-order skills such as analysis, evaluation and synthesis cannot be developed passively; they require deliberate effort and sustained self-regulation. Tutors are uniquely positioned to introduce and reinforce these expectations.

Starting Year 12 often also means meeting a new tutor at a time when everything, from buildings to **routines** to expectations, can feel unfamiliar. While this fresh start can be positive, it can also be unsettling. **Relationships** must therefore be built intentionally and quickly. Demonstrating interest, sharing small details about yourself and being consistently present signals to students that they are valued as whole people, not merely as exam candidates.

Ultimately, effective Key Stage 5 tutoring is about balancing guidance with respect, structure with agency and boundaries with explanation. By adopting this approach, tutors create a supportive environment that honours students' desire to be treated as emerging adults while equipping them with the understanding and habits required to succeed.

Stresses and Pressures

The pressures of Key Stage 5 begin almost as soon as students arrive. Level 3 qualifications, whether A levels, T Levels or BTEC Nationals, require a significant step up in academic challenge and personal responsibility. Students are expected to adapt quickly, often with limited transition support and little time to adjust to heightened expectations (Thompson, 2021). While substantial support is provided for the transition into Year 7, far less attention is given to preparing students for the equally demanding shift from Key Stage 4 to Key Stage 5. As a result, many enter sixth form facing a steep learning curve without the scaffolding earlier transitions received.

Many students feel underprepared for the independent study required at this stage. Coming from a more structured, teacher-led environment at GCSE, they often struggle with self-directed learning, managing longer assignments and planning without close supervision. City and Guilds Group (2017) shows that Level 3 vocational qualifications can be just as demanding as A-levels, requiring organisation, adaptability and reflection through industry placements and portfolio-based assessment.

Ofqual (2025) further emphasises the shift in cognitive demand: Level 2 qualifications prioritise recall, interpretation and basic application, while Level 3 requires students to engage with evaluation, synthesis and complex problem-solving – skills central to extended writing and critical thinking.

These higher expectations contribute to increased emotional and mental strain. Students frequently report anxiety around managing workload, meeting deadlines and adapting to greater independence, particularly in the first term of Year 12. Compounding this is the expectation that students begin planning their post-18 pathways – university, apprenticeships, employment or gap years – within the early months of Year 12. While necessary, this adds to an already heavy cognitive load at a time when many are still adjusting.

Pressure intensifies in Year 13. Coursework deadlines, mock exams and final assessments sit alongside major decisions about the future, which many students may not feel ready to make. Academic pressures are further compounded by external demands. Many students face parental expectations, or juggle part-time work. Household responsibilities, caring roles and driving lessons add further strain. These cumulative pressures can contribute to rising mental health concerns, particularly in Year 13. With expectations from school, family and themselves – and limited time to rest – many experience burnout, anxiety and a sense of barely keeping up. Year 13 can therefore feel like a perfect storm: Intense academic workload, high-stakes decisions and increasing outside responsibilities.

At the heart of managing these pressures is often the **relationships** between students and their form tutor. This daily connection – a familiar and **reliable** presence – allows tutors to notice early signs of difficulty, whether withdrawal, anxiety or overwhelm. Tutor time offers a consistent moment of calm within a fast-paced week: A space to pause, connect and reset. It can also serve as a place for low-stakes learning, where students engage in gentle cognitive warm-ups without assessment pressure. Inter-form quizzes, problem-solving tasks or short reflections activate thinking and support concentration, aligning with research showing that low-pressure retrieval improves readiness to learn (Sousa, 2016).

These activities also support wellbeing. Consistent relational **routines** help create psychological safety and emotional stability (Rimm-Kaufman and Sandilos, 2016). Structured pastoral sessions rooted in purposeful social–emotional learning also contribute to greater progress with academic outcomes (Education Endowment Foundation, 2025b). When planned intentionally, tutor time becomes a calm anchor in the school day, supporting reflection, connection and cognitive activation.

Crucially, the tutor's relational presence matters. Through everyday interactions and natural conversations, tutors can check in gently, notice when something is amiss and offer practical guidance, helping students break down overwhelming tasks, revisit study strategies or reframe challenges. A tutor's steady presence reassures students that they do not have to manage pressures alone and that support is available when needed. Often it is the tutor who recognises the quiet signs of struggle and offers early, sensitive intervention before difficulties escalate.

What to Expect From Behaviour

Key Stage 5 represents one of the biggest transitions in a young person's life. Students are moving from the relative structure of childhood into the freedoms and responsibilities associated with early adulthood. Developmental psychologists describe this period as emerging adulthood, a stage in which young people are no longer children but not yet fully adult, navigating increasing independence while still undergoing important cognitive and emotional development (Arnett, 2000). This in-between stage often leads to behaviours that can be confusing for both students and staff: Moments of maturity and independence followed by impulsivity, risk-taking and short-term decision-making.

Research into adolescent brain development helps explain this. During Key Stage 4, the brain's **reward** system becomes highly active, increasing sensitivity to peer influence, social acceptance and immediate gratification. By the time students enter Key Stage 5, this **reward** sensitivity is already well established. What continues to develop – and does so well into the early to mid-twenties – is the prefrontal cortex, the region responsible for planning, impulse control and long-term thinking (Casey, Jones and Hare, 2008). Steinberg (2010) explains that this developmental mismatch creates a dynamic where young people may understand long-term consequences intellectually yet still gravitate toward short-term **rewards** in practice. In other words, many sixth-form students know what they *should* do, but acting on that knowledge consistently remains challenging.

This is one of the reasons why the tutor period and the tutor–student **relationship** is so important at Key Stage 5. Left unstructured, tutor time can quickly become a space for socialising or procrastination, especially given the strong social motivations that persist from earlier adolescence. But when it has **routines** and **rigour**, tutor time becomes a safe and purposeful environment that sets the tone for the day.

Routines provide clarity and reduce opportunities for distraction. A structured programme, flexible enough to respond to the needs of the group yet consistent in ensuring each session has a meaningful activity, helps maintain focus and engagement. Whether tasks are completed independently, discussed with the tutor or explored collaboratively, this structure reduces off-task behaviour and fosters a calm, productive atmosphere. It also helps the group develop its own sense of identity, with shared activities such as debates, quizzes or reflective discussions strengthening connections and building a supportive community.

Rigour ensures that tutor activities feel purposeful rather than like 'filler', helping students recognise the value of engagement. For young people in emerging adulthood, who are still balancing long-term aspirations with immediate social or emotional **rewards**, this sense of purpose is essential. There will inevitably be times of pressure when students prefer to use tutor time for last-minute revision, and this can have its place, but when it becomes the default, tutor time risks being viewed as optional or simply a supervised gap. In providing structure, the tutor period becomes more than a routine; it becomes a daily anchor point where students feel guided, motivated and connected both to their studies and to the community around them. For Key Stage 5 students, it can also be a valuable opportunity to participate in the wider life of the school. Structured programmes such as reading buddies, peer mentoring or 'big brother/sister' schemes allow older students to meet regularly with younger pupils in Key Stage 3 or Key Stage 4, offering encouragement, academic support or simply a dependable point of contact. These roles not only benefit the younger students but also reinforce a sense of responsibility, confidence and belonging among sixth-formers. Likewise, taking part in inter-form competitions, quizzes or whole-school initiatives during tutor time helps Key Stage 5 students maintain their connection to the school community, fostering identity, leadership and collaboration beyond their academic studies.

However, **routines** and **rigour** only have impact when the tutor themselves is genuinely invested. Students quickly notice whether a tutor views the session as meaningful or merely administrative.

Enthusiasm, consistency and presence encourage positive engagement, modelling the commitment tutors hope to see in their students. When tutors prepare activities thoughtfully and participate fully, tutor time becomes more than a routine: It becomes a daily anchor of connection, guidance and support.

At its best, tutor time is far more than a slot on the timetable. It is a daily anchor, a chance to check in, build trust, foster resilience and reassure students that they are not navigating the complexities of emerging adulthood alone. Through consistency, care and clear purpose, tutors can make this time one of the most valuable aspects of a student's sixth form experience.

Ways to Support

Supporting students in Key Stage 5 begins with recognising that they are in a distinct developmental stage. They are emerging adults: No longer children, yet still developing the consistency, impulse control and long-term thinking associated with full adulthood (Steinberg, 2010). As a result, they often understand what is expected of them but may struggle to sustain the behaviours needed to meet those expectations, particularly when short-term **rewards** such as socialising or digital distractions compete with longer-term academic goals. The **6Rs** – **routines, relationships, rigour, reliable, rewards and receptive** – offer tutors a practical framework for guiding students through this stage.

Routines are especially powerful at Key Stage 5. Clear structures – daily check-ins, quizzes, reflective tasks or planned activities – help students manage distractions and settle quickly. Research shows that predictable **routines** reduce cognitive overload and support focus, particularly during periods of transition (Blakemore, 2018; Begeti, 2020). Alongside this, strong **relationships** remain essential. Positive tutor–student **relationships** are linked to better engagement, academic outcomes and emotional wellbeing (Rimm-Kaufman and Sandilos, 2016). Simple, consistent actions – learning names, noticing changes, showing interest – help build the trust that underpins effective pastoral support.

However, **relationships** must be accompanied by **rigour**. When tutor time lacks purpose, students disengage or assume it is less valuable than subject lessons. Thoughtful planning, meaningful activities and high expectations communicate that this time matters. Reliability reinforces this: Students need to know that their tutor is consistent, prepared and available, both in everyday **routines** and in moments of pastoral need. Reliability builds confidence and helps students feel secure during a demanding stage of education.

Rewards, though sometimes overlooked for older students, remain highly effective. Research into adolescent development shows that emerging adults are still sensitive to recognition and reinforcement (Steinberg, 2010). Small acknowledgements – verbal praise, positive messages home or informal celebration of achievements – can encourage positive habits and reinforce effort without feeling patronising.

Finally, **receptiveness** draws the **6Rs** together. Tutor groups differ widely, and students' needs evolve throughout Key Stage 5. Being adaptable, listening carefully and responding to the emerging priorities of the group shows students that their perspectives matter. When applied collectively, the **6Rs** transform tutor time from a gap in the timetable into a daily anchor point – a place of stability, trust and motivation that helps students thrive in sixth form.

Specific Challenges at This Key Stage

Being a tutor for Key Stage 5 students comes with a unique set of challenges, and perhaps the most significant is striking the right balance between academic mentoring and pastoral support. Sixth form students are under considerable pressure. Level 3 qualifications represent a steep step up in terms of academic **rigour** and the expectation of independent study. Tutors are often the first to notice when students begin to struggle, whether that is missing deadlines, losing motivation or becoming overwhelmed. In these moments, the tutor's role is not only to reinforce good study habits but also to provide reassurance and encouragement, showing students that setbacks are a natural part of the learning process.

This challenge is compounded by the fact that 16–19-year-olds are in a transitional stage of brain development. The prefrontal cortex, which governs planning, impulse control and long-term thinking, continues to mature well into the mid-twenties (Casey, Jones and Hare, 2008). Meanwhile, the brain's reward system is already highly developed, making adolescents particularly sensitive to short-term **rewards** such as socialising or screen time (Steinberg, 2010). This helps explain why some students thrive on the independence of sixth form, while others find it difficult to stay disciplined, particularly when faced with new experiences such as private study time, greater freedom or settling into an entirely new institution. For tutors, understanding this developmental stage allows for greater empathy and helps frame strategies that keep students engaged through **routines**, consistency and clear purpose.

Wellbeing is another key challenge. Recent research confirms that mental health difficulties are especially common among older adolescents. A mixed-methods study of high school students found that perceived stress levels were strongly linked to school-related pressures, including fear of failure, academic workload and concerns about future outcomes (John et al., 2025). Tutors, as the daily point of contact, are well placed to identify early signs of anxiety or withdrawal. Simple acts – checking in regularly, creating space for honest conversations and knowing when to signpost to professional support – can make a meaningful difference to a student's sense of being understood and cared for.

Finally, sixth form tutors often act as the first point of guidance for students' next steps, whether that involves university, apprenticeships or gap years. While no tutor can be expected to know everything, it is important to be informed about key processes such as UCAS, or at least to know where to direct students for impartial advice. The ability to combine pastoral care with practical guidance is what makes the Key Stage 5 tutor role so distinctive. At its best, it supports students not only academically but also in preparing for adulthood itself.

Conclusion

Tutoring at Key Stage 5 requires balancing academic mentoring with pastoral care, supporting students as they take on the increased independence and expectations of Level 3 study. Although the academic step-up from GCSEs can be challenging, clear **routines** and purposeful tutor activities can help students build confidence and develop effective habits. Structured elements such as weekly goal setting, study skills check-ins or short reflective tasks provide stability and help reduce procrastination by giving students predictable, focused ways to manage their workload.

Students' developing independence also means they benefit greatly from tutors who combine empathy with **rigour**. Purposeful tutor sessions signal that this time matters and ensure it supports the skills students need for success, whether managing deadlines, staying organised, or navigating moments of academic setback. When tutors communicate consistently, follow through on commitments and maintain high expectations, they help create a space where students feel supported both academically and personally.

Wellbeing remains a central focus at this stage. Sixth form students frequently experience pressure from workload, future planning and wider responsibilities. Tutors play an important preventative role by noticing early signs of stress or withdrawal and providing a **reliable** point of contact. Small, regular check-ins and a calm, consistent presence can help students feel grounded and seen, while timely signposting ensures specialist help is available when needed.

Finally, the tutor period supports students as they make decisions about their post-18 pathways. While tutors do not need to hold all the answers, being approachable, informed and ready to direct students to suitable guidance ensures they receive the impartial support they need at key moments. When tutor sessions are responsive and rooted in genuine partnership, they become more than a daily formality: They provide an anchor point where academic progress, wellbeing and future aspirations can be supported together.

- Embed routines with purpose: Use structured, consistent activities such as study skills check-ins, weekly goals or reflective tasks to encourage productive habits and reduce procrastination.
- Balance academic and pastoral support: Be proactive in spotting when students are struggling and use tutor time to model strategies for managing pressure, setbacks and organisation.
- Prioritise wellbeing: Look for early signs of stress or withdrawal. Build trust through reliability, small daily check-ins and clear communication, and signpost to specialist support where appropriate.
- Foster receptiveness and student voice: Treat tutor time as a partnership. Listen, adapt activities to your group and show genuine investment in their academic, personal and future development.

References and Bibliography

Arnett, J. J. (2000) 'Emerging adulthood: A theory of development from the late teens through the twenties', *American Psychologist*, 55(5), pp. 469–480.

Begeti, F. (2020) 'Metacognition and learning in adolescence: Developmental considerations', *Educational and Developmental Psychologist*, 37(2), pp. 108–117.

Blakemore, S-J. (2018) *Inventing ourselves: The secret life of the teenage brain.* Transworld.

Casey, B. J., Jones, R. M. and Hare, T. A. (2008) 'The adolescent brain', *Annals of the New York Academy of Sciences*, 1124(1), pp. 111–126. Available at: https://pubmed.ncbi.nlm.nih.gov/18400927/ (Accessed 31 January 2026).

City and Guilds (2017) *People power: Does the UK have the right skills for the future?* Available at: https://www.businessboardnetwork.co.uk/media/1900/people-power-city-guilds-group.pdf (Accessed 29 January 2026).

Education Endowment Foundation (2025a) *Metacognition and self-regulated learning: Guidance report.* Available at: https://d2tic4wvo1iusb.cloudfront.net/production/eef-guidance-reports/metacognition/metacognition-and-self-regulated-learning_guidance-report.v.2.4.0.pdf (Accessed 30 January 2026).

Education Endowment Foundation (2025b) *Social and emotional learning.* Available at: https://educationendowmentfoundation.org.uk/education-evidence/teaching-learning-toolkit/social-and-emotional-learning (Accessed 31 January 2026).

John, D., Ottmann, S., Rechberger, K-H., O'Rourke, T., Pryss, R. and Probst, T. (2025) 'Quality of life, perceived stress, and use of school-based stress management interventions in high school students: A mixed-methods study during and after COVID-19', *Frontiers in Public Health,* 13. Available at https://doi.org/10.3389/fpubh.2025.1658346 (Accessed 29 January 2026).

Ofqual (2025) *Ofqual handbook: General conditions of recognition.* Available at: https://www.gov.uk/guidance/ofqual-handbook/section-e-design-and-development-of-qualifications (Accessed 31 January 2026).

Rimm-Kaufman, S. E. and Sandilos, L. E. (2016). *Improving students' relationships with teachers to provide essential supports for learning.* Available at https://www.apa.org/education-career/k12/relationships (Accessed 31 January 2026).

Shinwell, J. and Defeyter, M. A. (2017) 'Investigating the impact of summer learning loss on children's reading', *Frontiers in Education*, 2(11), pp. 1–9.

Sousa, D. (2016) *How the brain learns.* 5th edition. Corwin.

Steinberg, L. (2010) 'A dual systems model of adolescent risk-taking', *Developmental Psychobiology*, 52(3), pp. 216–224.

Taverner, S. et al. (2001) 'Students' transition between Key Stage 4 and post-16 learning', *British Journal of Educational Studies*, 49(4), pp. 498–512.

Thompson, M. (2021) 'Navigating entry into higher education: The transition to independent learning and living'. Available at https://pure.hartpury.ac.uk/ws/files/46544099/Navigating_entry_into_higher_education_the_transition_to_independent_learning_and_living.pdf (Accessed 12 January 2026).

Conclusion

Sophie-Lauren McPhee

Thank you for picking up this book – you are clearly equally passionate as we all are about the role of form tutoring, or are convinced that others can be persuaded to be. You have seen that a form tutor is far more than an administrative assistant: They are leadership cultivators, safeguarding frontline personnel and community builders. By picking up this book you know that teenagers will remember their best form tutors for a very long time, if not for the rest of their lives, and that a good secondary school form tutor is a strong and sturdy ship that guides pupils from being children into legal adults.

You've read about the centrality of the **6Rs** to the role of form tutor and how they provide the scaffolding upon which successful days, weeks, months and years at school are built. However, what happens in each classroom and around the school is heavily dependent on the whole school culture – it's all very well if you are religiously implementing the **6Rs**, but unless there is strong school leadership, parent/carer buy-in and consistency across staff, your good work can only go so far. There needs to be visual reminders around school and frequent communication of school values to the pupil, staff, parent and governor bodies, so that what you are doing is part of a cohesive whole. Could the **6Rs** even form part of your pupils' vocabulary? Could they be displayed? Could they be explored as part of assemblies or tutor time? Explicitly naming what you are doing and the pupils' role in return will help bring the community together in shared pursuit and social harmony.

Maybe there is a member of your Senior Leadership Team (SLT) who has overall responsibility for school culture – it would be worth a chat to them. I worked in schools across the UK as part of my Change

DOI: 10.4324/9781003620976-12

Your Mind peer education programme, and the best-functioning schools were those where culture and values permeated the building: Values were explicitly named, **routines** were visible throughout and rigorously enforced, and there was a real sense of togetherness. If you aspire to this role one day, now is the time to start working towards it, by consciously building and nurturing the culture within your form group. You could insist that one of your performance management (PM) targets is related to the role of form tutor – or better still, speak to your Headteacher about all staff having one PM target related to pastoral work! At the end of the day, academic grades are, of course, important, but if we are not cultivating healthy, happy, safe, pro-social human beings, then I think we are missing the point of what makes a good education.

This last point is why schools need to also have an eye on educating parents and carers too. In the past, in my role as Mental Health Week Coordinator, I have hosted the Charlie Waller Trust to deliver excellent free-of-charge talks on the adolescent brain and teenage mental health. In my experience, some parents and carers struggle to adapt to the changes in their children as they move through secondary school, and need to be carefully reminded that when their child is metaphorically pulling away from them, that this is not only normal, but developmentally necessary. Of course, as a form tutor, this would go way beyond the remit of your role, but if you are ever talking to a parent on the telephone or at parents' evening, my experience is that a lot of empathy and a little bit of gentle educating goes a long way. However, if you ever find yourself out of your depth, the benefit of being 'just' a form tutor is that you can – and should – pass on any tricky issues to your Head of Year or a member of SLT.

Although form tutoring is a seriously important role, it's a seriously fun one, too. They might be in secondary school, but don't assume they are too old for stuff we might normally associate with primary school pupils. In my time, I have used the designated reading time to read novels aloud to my form – with some even bringing blankets, milk and cookies for the occasion! Even the normally challenging teens have enjoyed the opportunity to channel their inner toddler and forget about the stress of adolescence for even 15 minutes, reminiscing about a simpler time. I have arranged Secret Santas (with homemade items only, to avoid financial pressure and encourage meaningful gift-giving) and an advent calendar with teddy-bear chocolates inside. (I worked in an all-boys' school, I hasten to add). We can forget sometimes that not only are they still children, but that the inner child resides in all of us – even worn-out teachers! So, having fun with your form is good for you too.

And what of the future of form tutoring? Well, in an age where some might avoid the three-week wait for a GP appointment by typing their ailments into an AI platform, where clients turn up in therapy rooms to talk about what they've read on social media about how to navigate their relationship, and people are turning to chatbots to fill the void where a partner may have once been, you could be forgiven for thinking that the role of form tutor will soon be redundant. Yet the opposite is true: Your job is to resist this tide of increasing isolation and technological dependency and push for more human connection. When you are overwhelmed by planning, marking and admin, as so many teachers are, it is tempting to let them chat while you squeeze another few minutes of emails in. However, not only are you not actually reducing your overwhelm – how much can you really get done in tutor time anyway? – you are making the job less pleasurable: Many teachers say that interacting with the pupils is the best part of the job. And these minutes might feel like a sacrifice to you when there's a few quick jobs you could be getting on with, but to one pupil in your form, they could be the best minutes of their day.

So, I say to you: Resist. Resist the other jobs you have to do, resist the 'always on' culture, resist the technology that encourages us away from real **relationships**. The richness of this career does not come from marking a set of exercise books, nor the salary. It comes from all the quirky, quiet, loud, compliant, rebellious, wonderful children you have the opportunity to get to know. Savour it! You have been given the privilege of being those children's primary nurturer in school – that is far more important than any scheme of work and any examination result. So, good luck to you and thank you, form tutors, for all the little things you do to make children feel seen, welcomed and safe. Let's work together to help others see what form tutoring is: The most important job in school.

Index

For Product Safety Concerns and Information please contact our EU representative GPSR@taylorandfrancis.com
Taylor & Francis Verlag GmbH, Kaufingerstraße 24, 80331 München, Germany

www.ingramcontent.com/pod-product-compliance
Lightning Source LLC
LaVergne TN
LVHW061723260926
848956LV00030B/263
* 9 7 8 1 0 4 1 0 2 7 8 7 4 *